MANGA UNIVERSITY presents...

The Comic Book That Teaches You How To Read And Write Japanese!

Japanime

TOKYO SAN FRANCISCO

Manga University presents ... Kanji de Manga
The Comic Book That Teaches You
How To Read And Write Japanese!
Volume One

ISBN 4-921205-02-7

Published by Japanime Co. Ltd.
3-31-18 Nishi-Kawaguchi
Kawaguchi-shi, Saitama 332-0021
Japan

First edition December 2004
Second edition October 2005

Printed in Japan

The Manga University Mission Statement

The mission of Manga University is to enlighten and educate the international community on all aspects of Japanese culture through the creative use of traditional manga artwork.

The University recognizes that manga transcends mainstream entertainment and possesses a unique ability to convey the true spirit of Japan, making the art form an ideal communicative tool to touch the lives and inspire the minds of Japan enthusiasts worldwide.

Our mission and philosophy are firmly rooted in the principles and conviction of the Japanese educational tradition and in the best ideals of Japanese heritage.

Founded at the turn of the century and located in Tokyo, Manga University is one of the world's foremost publishers of manga-themed educational materials.

CONTENTS

FOREWORD

Students are usually taught that the easiest way to memorize kanji is to think of the characters as little pictures of the objects, actions and ideas they represent. For instance, the kanji for "tree," 木, really does look like a tree trunk with a couple of outstretched branches, and 山 does sort of resemble a mountain.

But what about the hundreds of other everyday kanji you will need to know if you want to read a menu, map or manga in Japanese? Can anyone honestly say 食 really looks like "food," 行 obviously means "to go," or 友 reminds you of a "friend"? So much for simplicity!

"Kanji de Manga" takes a refreshingly different approach. Instead of relying on tired, outdated memory aids, the authors introduce kanji in an exciting format millions of young people can't seem to get enough of: Japanese comics. Each page features a manga drawing with fun dialog showing a single kanji character "in action." An English translation of the comic strip helps reinforce the reader's vocabulary, stroke order is demonstrated step-by-step, and useful compounds are also provided.

By learning how to read and write the 80 kanji presented in this volume, you will have taken the first step toward mastering the Japanese writing system. So don't bother with the "little pictures." Look at the BIGGER pictures—the manga on the pages of this exciting book—and memorize kanji today!

Tomonori Morikawa, Ph.D.
Professor, School of International Liberal Studies
Waseda University
Tokyo, Japan

INTRODUCTION

When you opened this book, you opened the doorway to a new frontier. That frontier is kanji, and it holds the key to reading and writing the Japanese language.

At first, these characters may look difficult, mysterious and even a little intimidating. But "Kanji de Manga" is here to help sort it all out for you in a simple, fun way.

There are nearly 50,000 kanji. You could literally spend a lifetime learning kanji and still not know every character. But don't give up hope just yet. Even most native speakers of Japanese know only a fraction of these 50,000 kanji by heart.

In fact, Japanese students are required to learn just 2,000 of those characters. You need to know only about half of those to read the typical Japanese newspaper—and even less than that to

be able to read your favorite manga books in the original Japanese.

Of course, that still leaves plenty to learn, especially when you compare all those characters to the mere 26 letters of the English alphabet. But "Kanji de Manga" contains everything you need to get started, and hopefully you'll have a little fun along the way, too.

By the time you reach the end of this book, you'll be able to read and write the 80 kanji featured in Level 4, the most basic level, of the Japanese Language Proficiency Test. (For more information about the test, please see page 94.) These are the same characters studied in Japan by first- and second-grade students, and include some of the most common and important kanji that you will need to know.

Before we begin, let's take a quick look at the origins of kanji.

Kanji is based on the ancient Chinese writing system. In many cases, these characters are still in use today in China. But don't try to learn both languages at once: While some kanji share the same meaning in both languages, many do not, and the sentence structures of the two languages are profoundly different.

Most kanji have at least two common pronunciations: a purely Japanese pronunciation, called kun-yomi, and one based on the original Chinese, called on-yomi. The Japanese began borrowing kanji many centuries ago, so the on-yomi pronunciations—Japanese versions of Middle Chinese—usually sound very different from the modern Chinese pronunciation of each character.

You will find both pronunciations in this book. Like many Japanese-language textbooks, we will show you the kun-yomi in hiragana and on-yomi in katakana. And if you haven't gotten your hiragana and katakana down yet, don't worry—simply get out your copy of "Kana de Manga" for a quick refresher.

You may have noticed that we said that each character has *at least* two pronunciations. Some characters have even more. Many of those are obscure and seldom-used pronunciations, and we have omitted them from this lesson to help move things along. You won't miss them!

Even when we narrow each character down to its two most common pronunciations, figuring out whether to use the on-yomi or kun-yomi can still be tricky. At first, it may seem random and unstructured. And, in some ways, it is.

But soon you'll begin to notice some trends. Compound words, or words made up of multiple kanji, are generally read using the on-yomi pronunciation. Kanji occurring in isolation, or next to only kana characters, are generally read using the kun-yomi pronunciation. Japanese place names and family names also tend to be pronounced using the kun-yomi pronunciations.

There are, of course, exceptions—and plenty of them. In fact, the very name of the country—Japan—is read using the on-yomi pronunciation: "Nihon," or 日本 in kanji. And when it comes to given names, even native speakers often need a little help trying to figure it all out.

But don't be daunted. The task may be difficult, and the journey long, but with "Kanji de Manga" as your guide, you'll also find it rewarding and fun.

So let's get started on the journey of a lifetime—a journey into the magical world of Japanese culture. And when you are ready to graduate to the next level, "Kanji de Manga" will be ready to take the next step with you with our more advanced lessons.

Ready? Set? Gambatte!

PAGE GUIDE

① The featured kanji

② Common definition

③ Readings: kun-yomi (Japanese readings) are written in hiragana, while on-yomi (Chinese readings) are in katakana.

④ Examples of compounds containing the featured kanji, their pronunciations (written in hiragana) and English definitions. (An asterisk next to a compound indicates that one or more of its kanji are not featured in this volume of the "Kanji de Manga" series.)

⑤ Stroke order: In general, the strokes are written from top to bottom and left to right. For a list of additional stroke-order rules, please refer to the chart at the back of this book.

⑥ The manga. All dialogue is written in hiragana and katakana except for the single featured kanji. The proper pronunciation of the kanji is indicated in furigana (tiny hiragana) written above the character.

⑦ Translation of the dialogue and selected onomatopoeia.

STUDY SECTION

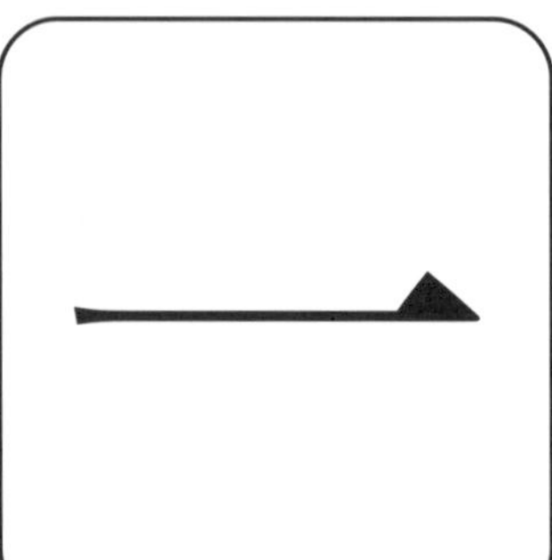

ONE

ひと、ひと(つ)、イチ、イッ

ex. 一つ (ひとつ) - one (object)

ex. 一月 (いちがつ) - January

だっ　たたた　だだだだ
(Onomatopoeia for the sound of heavy footsteps or running. Onomatopoeia are very common in the Japanese language and especially in manga, and can be found throughout this book.)

一ちゃくっ！
First place!

TWO

ふた、ふた(つ)、ニ

ex. 二つ (ふたつ) - two (objects)

ex. 二月 (にがつ) - February

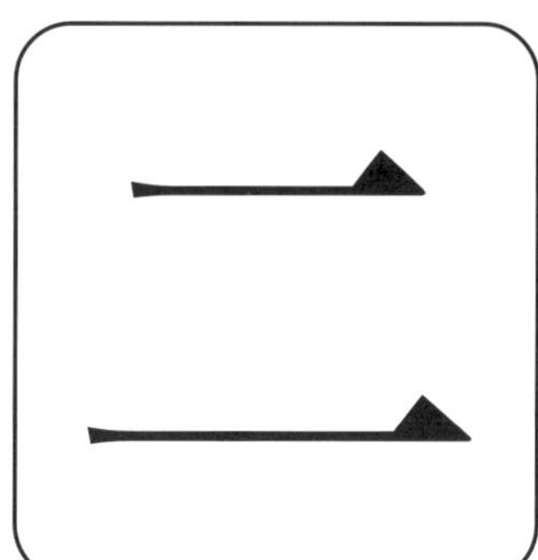

Mother: しゃしんとるわよ。
いちたすいちは？
Time for a photo.
One plus one equals?

Children: 二！
Two!

(In Japan, it is common for children to flash two fingers—in the "V for Victory" sign—when posing for photographs.)

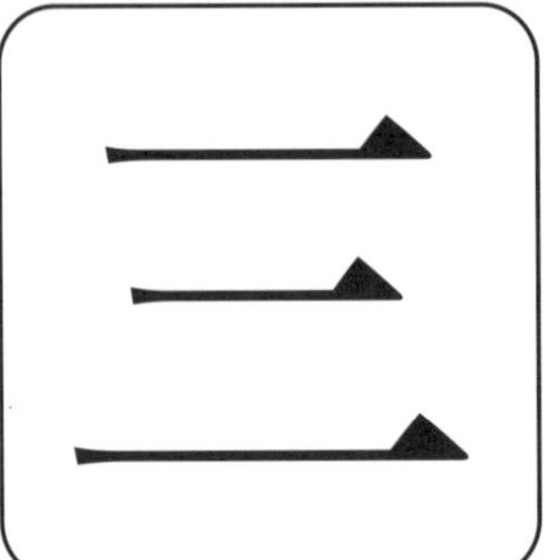

THREE

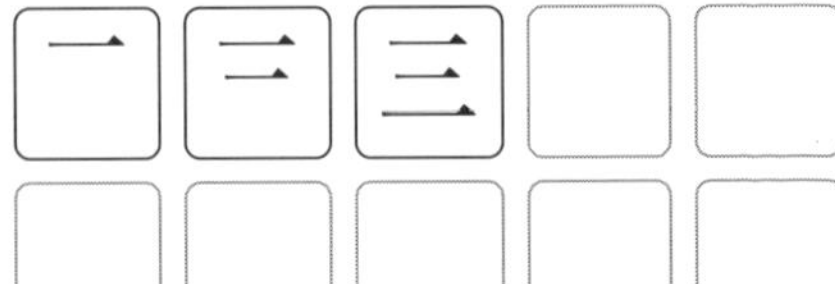

ex. 三つ (みっつ) - three (objects)

ex. 三月 (さんがつ) - March

Schoolboy: 三じって
たのしみなんだ。
I can't wait till 3 o'clock!

Schoolgirl: なぜ？
Why's that?

Schoolboy: 三じといえばおやつの
じかんだろ! はやくならないかな？
Because 3 o'clock is snack time!
Is it time yet?

Schoolgirl: キラキラしてる...
There are stars in his eyes...

FOUR

よ、よ(つ)、よっ(つ)、よん、シ

ex. 四つ (よっつ) - four (objects)

ex. 四月 (しがつ) - April

Girl: わ、四つばのクローバー。なにかいいことがありそう…
Wow, a four-leaf clover! I think I've got some luck heading my way...

Boy: すみません。ハンカチをおとされましたよ。はい、どうぞ。
Excuse me. You dropped your hanky. Here you go.

Girl: かっこいい！あたらしいこいのよかん！
He's so cute! I think I'm in love!

FIVE

いつ、いつ(つ)、ゴ

ex. 五つ (いつつ) - five (objects)
ex. 五月 (ごがつ) - May

Boy: 五ほんのわかれみち。
どれをいこうかなぁ。
Five different roads.
Which one should I take?

SIX

む、む(つ)、むっ(つ)、むい、ロク

ex. 六つ (むっつ) - six (objects)

ex. 六月 (ろくがつ) - June

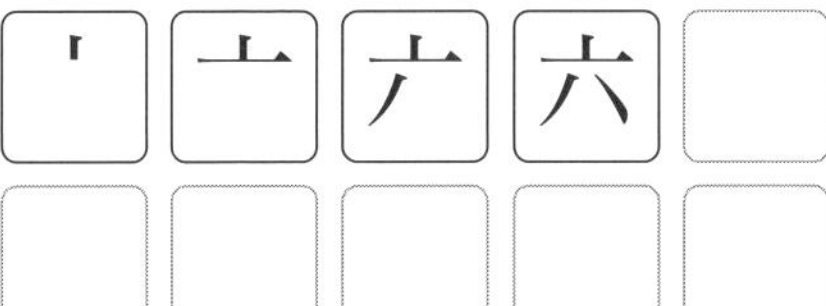

Girl: わぁ… ゆきの けっしょうって、
Ah, falling snowflakes...

きれいな六かっけい！
...are beautiful hexagons!

SEVEN

なな、なな(つ)、なの、シチ

ex. 七つ (ななつ) - seven (objects)
ex. 七月 (しちがつ) - July

Boy: 七ってえんぎのいいすうじだな。
Seven is a lucky number, right?

ラッキーセブン。
Lucky seven.

七ふくじん。
The Seven Gods of Fortune.

(The "Shichifukujin" are Ebisu [god of commerce], Daikokuten [wealth], Bishamonten [warriors], Hotei [abundance], Benzaiten [music] Fukurokuju [wisdom] and Juroujin [longevity].)

EIGHT

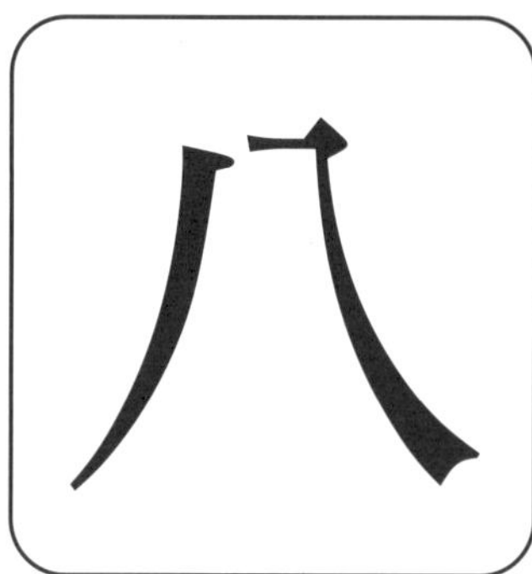

や、や(つ)、やっ(つ)、よう、ハチ

ex. 八つ (やっつ) - eight (objects)
ex. 八月 (はちがつ) - August

Boy: もうすこしたべたいけど…
I'd like to eat a bit more, but...

Boy: はら八ぶんめっていうし、
やめておこう！ごちそうさま。
They say a stomach that is only 80% full is best, so I better stop! Delicious!

Mother: そんなにたべて？
(Only 80% full) after eating all that?

NINE

ここの、ここの(つ)、キュウ、ク

ex. 九つ (ここのつ) - nine (objects)
ex. 九月 (くがつ) - September

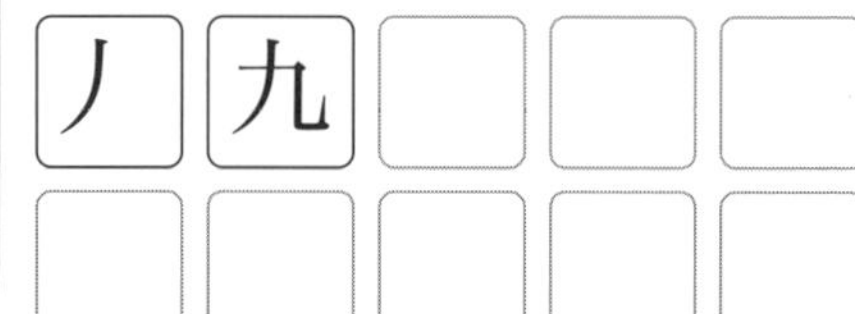

Radio announcer: おおっと！
ピッチャーおいつめられた！
九かいのうら２アウト…
The pitcher is in a jam.
Bottom of the 9th, 2 outs...

…まんるい！
...and the bases are loaded!

TEN

とお、と、ジュウ、ジッ

ex. 十 (とお) - ten (objects)

ex. 十月 (じゅうがつ) - October

ばんっ (sound of door slam)

Mother: おきなさい！
あさよ！
Wake up! It's morning!

Son: えー…
Huh?

ゔーん (thump)

Son: あと十ぷんだけねかせて。おねがい…
Let me sleep another 10 minutes. Please...

Mother: がっこうちこくするわよ。
おきなさい！
You'll be late for school. Get up now!

HUNDRED

ヒャク、ビャク、ピャク

ex. 百円 (ひゃくえん) - ¥100

ex. 百万 (ひゃくまん) - one million

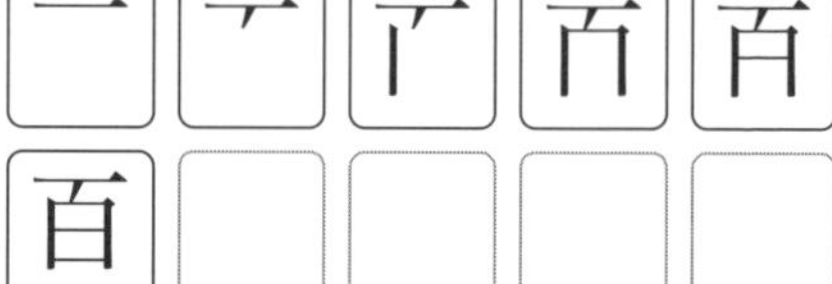

Babysitter: もう…
Ugh...

Boy: おかしかって、かって、かってー！
Buy me some candy!

Babysitter: 百えんまでよ！
OK, but only 100 yen.

Boy: わーい！
Yay!

THOUSAND

ち、セン、ゼン

ex. 千年 (せんねん) - millennium

ex. 千円 (せんえん) - ¥1,000

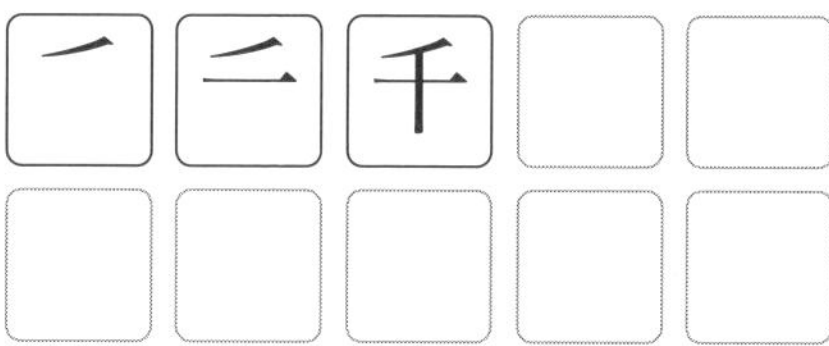

Big sister: なにをつくっているの？おりがみ？
What are you making? Origami?

Little sister: 千ばづるよ。がんかけするのよ。
I'm making a thousand paper cranes. It's for good luck!

Big sister: すごい！
Wow!

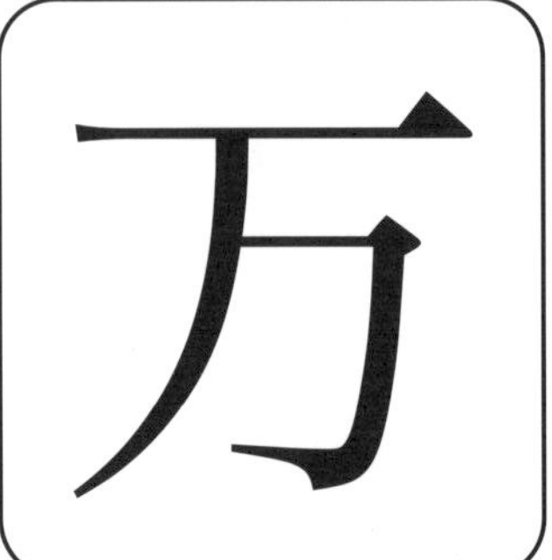

TEN THOUSAND

マン、バン

ex. 一万円 (いちまんえん) - ¥10,000
ex. 万国 (ばんこく) - the whole world

Athlete: いち万ぽめざしてあるくの
がんばるぞ！
I'm going to walk 10,000 steps!

Cheerleader: おー！
Right on!

Athlete: も…もうだめ…
That's it...I'm beat...

Cheerleader: まだ5ふんしか
たっていないでしょ！
It's only been five minutes!

CIRCLE / YEN

まる(い)、エン

ex. 十円 (じゅうえん) - ¥10
ex. 円い (まるい) - round, circular

Store clerk: ごうけい…2,000円のおかいあげです。
Your total comes to...2,000 yen.

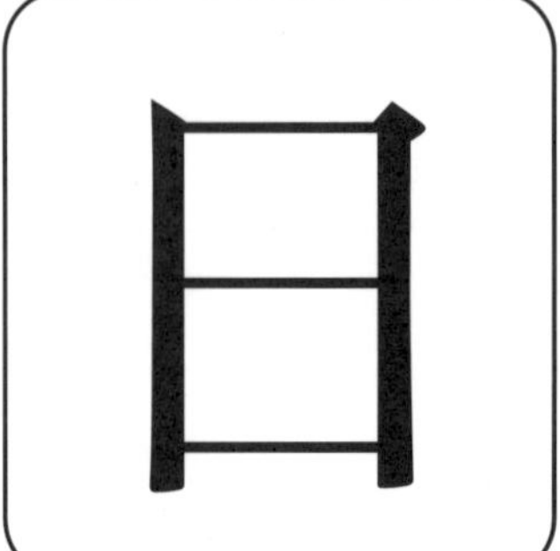

SUN / DAY

ひ、か、び、ニチ、ジツ

ex. 日の出 (ひので) - sunrise
ex. 日曜日* (にちようび) - Sunday

Girl: 日のでのうみ。
日のいりのうみ。
Sunrise at the beach.
Sunset at the beach.

Girl: どちらもすてき。
Both are beautiful.

Boy: (speechless)

MOON / MONTH

つき、ゲツ、ガツ

ex. 毎月 (まいつき) - every month

ex. 月曜日* (げつようび) - Monday

Father: 月にはうさぎがすんでいるんだよ。

You know, rabbits live on the moon.

Children (in unison): ほんとー？すげー。ステキ。

Really? Wow! How romantic!

(While Westerners say they can see the face of a man on the moon, Japanese claim to see the image of a rabbit making rice cakes.)

FIRE

ひ、び、カ

ex. 花火* (はなび) - fireworks
ex. 火曜日* (かようび) - Tuesday

Girls: ふゆのだいごみといえば…
The best thing about winter...

Girls: たき火でヤキイモよね！おいしいね。
Roasting sweet potatoes on an open fire! Delicious!

WATER

みず、スイ

ex. 飲み水 (のみみず) - drinking water

ex. 水曜日* (すいようび) - Wednesday

だだだ だだだ だだだ
(sound of heavy running)

ぜーはー ぜーはー ぜーはー (panting)

Boy: た…ただいま。み…水をいっぱいちょうだい。

I...I'm home. Gimme lots of wa...water.

Mother: うわ… はい、どうぞ。

Yikes! Here you go!

TREE / WOOD

き、ぎ、こ、ボク、モク

ex. 木登り* (きのぼり) - tree-climbing
ex. 木曜日* (もくようび) - Thursday

Boy on left: うわぁー。
Wow!

Boy on right: 木のうえからのながめってさいこう！
The view from the top of this tree is awesome!

GOLD / MONEY

かね、かな、キン、コン

ex. お金 (おかね) - money (polite form)

ex. 金曜日* (きんようび) - Friday

Boy: うわー！ほしかった ゲームだ！
Wow! It's that game I've been wanting to buy!

ほしいけど、お金がたりるかな。しんぱい。
I really want to get it, but I wonder if I have enough money on me.

SOIL / GROUND

つち、ド、ト

ex. 土地* (とち) - a plot of land
ex. 土曜日* (どようび) - Saturday

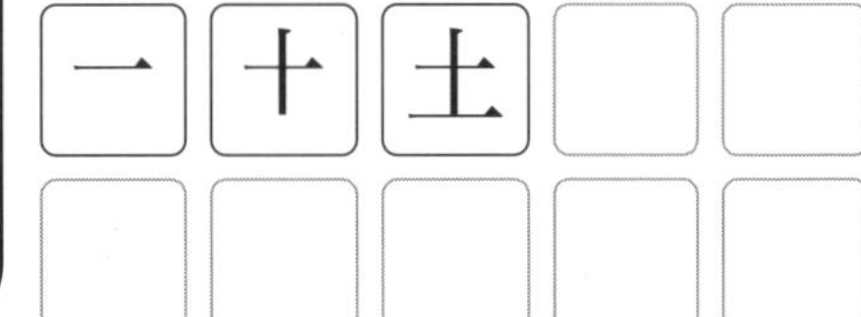

Man: てつだうって
いったけど…
いったけど…
I know I said I'd help, but...

Man: こんなにひろい土ちをたがやすの？
ひろすぎるよー！
We have to plow this whole field?
It's TOO big!

Farmer: うん。そう。
Yep. Yessiree.

MINUTE

わ(ける)、わ(かる)、ブン、フン、ブ

ex. 一分 (いっぷん) - one minute
ex. 分かる (わかる) - to understand

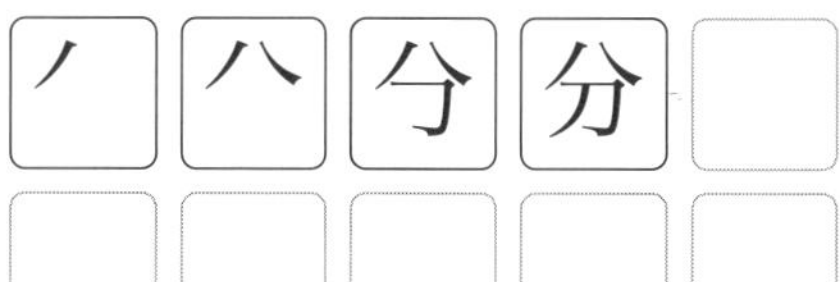

トポポ…
(sound of water being poured)

ちらっ (sound of boy looking at clock)

Boy: カップラーメンというのは、できあがるまでのすう分がまちどおしいな。
It's those few minutes of anticipation while it cooks that make instant ramen taste so good!

TIME

とき、ジ

ex. 時計* (とけい) - watch, clock

ex. 一時 (いちじ) - one o'clock

Schoolgirl: もうこんな時かん。どうしようー。
Look at the time.
I'm gonna be in trouble.

Mother: いまなん時だとおもっているの！？おそくまであそんでばかり！べんきょうもしなさい！
Do you know what time it is!? Quit playing around all the time! Do some studying for a change!

INTERVAL

あいだ、ま、カン、ケン

ex. 時間 (じかん) - time
ex. 中間 (ちゅうかん) - midway
ex. 人間 (にんげん) - human

Boy (reaching into a storm drain): すき間におかねをおとしちゃった。も…もうすこし…
My coin fell into this little space. Ju...just a little bit more...

YEAR

とし、ネン

ex. 今年 (ことし) - this year
ex. 去年* (きょねん) - last year

Girl: おかあさん、年れいいくつになったの？プリントにかくのよ。
Mom, how old will you be this year? I need to put your age on this form.

Mother: 28さいと276かげつよ。
28 years and 276 months。

Girl: (speechless)

THIS / NOW

いま、コン

ex. 今日 (きょう) - this day; today
ex. 今月 (こんげつ) - this month

はははははははは
(boy laughing at comic book)

Mother: しゅくだいは
おわったの？
Have you finished your homework?

Boy: 今するところ！
I was just about to start now!

あせ あせ あせ
(sound of quick movement)

EVERY

マイ

ex. 毎日 (まいにち) - every day
ex. 毎月 (まいつき) - every month

Student: よーし！きょうから
毎にちにっきをつけるぞー！
All right! Beginning today, I'm going to keep a diary every day!

BEFORE

まえ、ゼン

ex. 五分前 (ごふんまえ) - five minutes ago
ex. 前日 (ぜんじつ) - the day before

Boy: あ、いたいた。
Ah, there she is!

Girl: 前にきをつけて！
Watch out in front of you!

ぶっ (thump)

Girl: —— *(inaudible)*!

Boy: え？きこえない。
What? I can't hear you.

NOON

ゴ

ex. 午前 (ごぜん) - a.m.
ex. 午後 (ごご) - p.m.

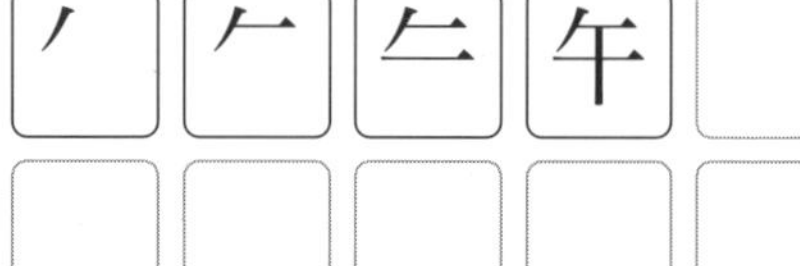

Schoolboy: がっこうは
午ぜんちゅうでおわり。
School ends at noon today.

午ごは…あそぶぞ！
This afternoon...I'm gonna have fun!

HALF

なか(ば)、ハン

ex. 一時半 (いちじはん) - 1:30
ex. 半年 (はんとし) - half a year

Boy: あーん…
Yum!

たべたい？
You want to eat some too?

わん (dog's "woof")

半ぶんこ。
OK, half each.

WHAT?

なに、なん

ex. 何時 (なんじ) - what time?
ex. 何人 (なんにん) - how many people?

Sister: どうしたの？
What's wrong?

何をいっているのかわからないわ…
I have no idea what he's saying...

AFTER / BACK

のち、うし(ろ)、あと、ゴ、ゴウ

ex. 二日後 (ふつかご) - two days later

ex. 後ろ (うしろ) - behind

Boy: 後はオレにどーんとまかせてよ！
どーんと。
Leave the rest up to me! I'll take care of it.

Girl: ありがとう。
Thanks.

どん (chest-thumping)

ゲホゲホゲホッ
(coughing)

Girl: だいじょうぶかしら。
ふあんだわ。
I hope things will be OK.
I'm a bit worried now.

AHEAD

さき、セン

ex. 先月 (せんげつ) - last month

ex. 先生 (せんせい) - teacher

わー…
おばけやしき
だって。
う…ん。
おばけやしき
おまえが
先(さき)にいけよ。
いやいや、
先(さき)にどうぞ。

First boy: わー… おばけやしきだって。 Hey, it's the haunted house.

Second boy: う…ん。 Yeah.

First boy: おまえが先にいけよ。 You go first.

Second boy: いやいや、先にどうぞ。 Nah, that's all right. You go first.

Witch: はやくはいってこないかなー。 I wish they'd hurry up and come inside!

HIGH / EXPENSIVE

たか、たか(い)、コウ

ex. 高すぎる (たかすぎる) - too expensive

ex. 高校 (こうこう) - high school

First boy: えー！
バンジージャンプ？！
Huh? You're gonna bungee-jump?!

Second boy: そうよ。
That's right.

Second boy: 高しょきょうふしょうなのに。
But I'm terrified of high places!

ガタ ガタ ガタ
(sound of knees knocking)

NORTH

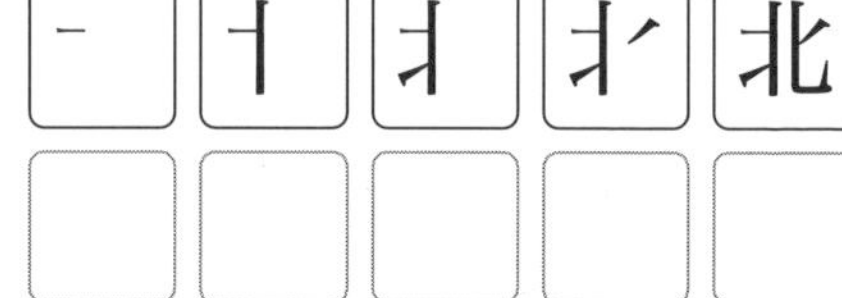

きた、ホク

ex. 北口* (きたぐち) - north entrance
ex. 北米* (ほくべい) - North America

Businessman: きょうは
いちだんと…
Today in particular…

くしゅん
(sound of sneezing)

北かぜがつよいなぁ。
…the wind from the north is strong.

ビュー
(sound of a strong wind)

SOUTH

みなみ、ナン

ex. 南口* (みなみぐち) - south entrance
ex. 南米* (なんべい) - South America

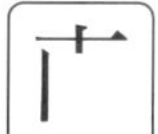

Sunbather: リゾートといえば、やはり南のしまにかぎるな。
When you think of a paradise resort, it's gotta be on an island in the south.
きもちいいなぁ。さいこうだよ。
I feel great. It's beautiful.

EAST

ひがし、トウ

ex. 東口* (ひがしぐち) - east entrance
ex. 東京* (とうきょう) - Tokyo

Teacher: はい、みなさん。たいようは…
OK, everyone. The sun...

Students (in unison): 東からのぼります！
Rises from the east!

Teacher: はい！
That's correct!

WEST

にし、セイ、サイ

ex. 西口* (にしぐち) - west entrance
ex. 西洋* (せいよう) - Western countries

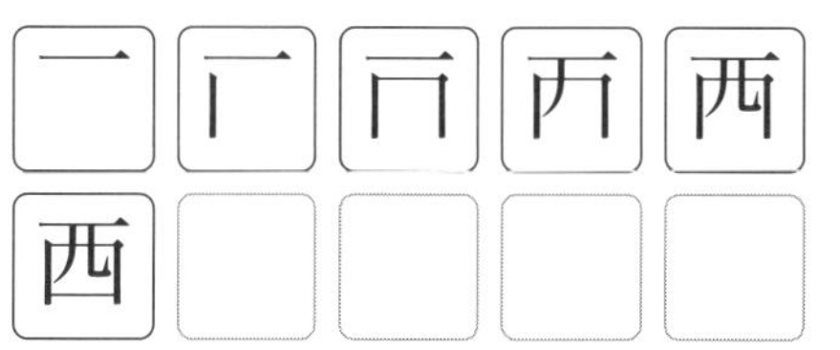

First boy: (speechless)

Second boy: わっ、
はんぶんだけ
ひやけしてる？！
Yikes! Why are you sunburned on just one side of your body?!

First boy: 西びばかりあびて
このとおりさ。
I sat facing the west all day.

Second boy: なるほど。
That explains it.

UP / ABOVE

うえ、あ(げ)る、あ(が)る、ジョウ

ex. 年上 (としうえ) - elder
ex. 上下 (じょうげ) - up and down

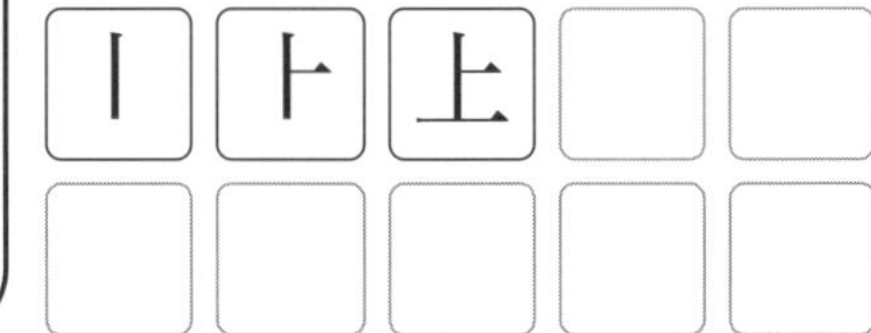

Big brother: おーい
Hey!

キョロ キョロ
(sound of head turning left and right)

Little brother: ここだよー。
Here I am.

Big brother: なんだ。上にいたのか。
Oh, you're up there!

DOWN / UNDER

した、くだ、さ(げ)る、カ、ゲ

ex. 年下 (としした) - junior
ex. 下さい (ください) - please

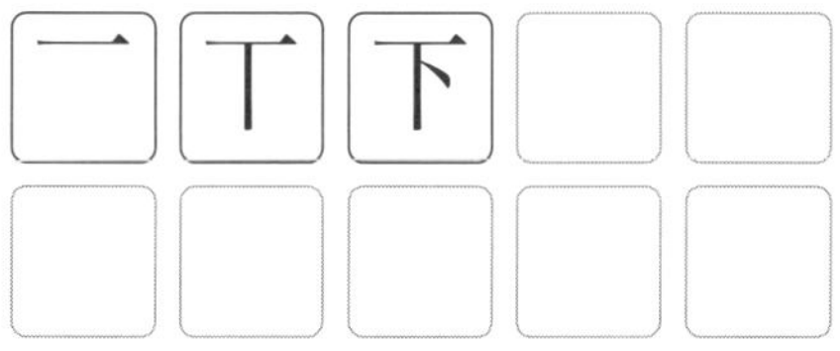

Big boy: 下には、いろいろな
ものがうまっているんだよ。
There are many things buried
under the ground.

Little boy: へー。
Really?

LEFT

ひだり、サ

ex. 左側* (ひだりがわ) - left-hand side
ex. 左右 (さゆう) - either side

First boy: 左ききなんだね。
So, you're a lefty.

Second boy: うん。
Yep.

RIGHT

みぎ、ウ、ユウ

ex. 右側* (みぎがわ) - right-hand side
ex. 右巻き* (みぎまき) - clockwise

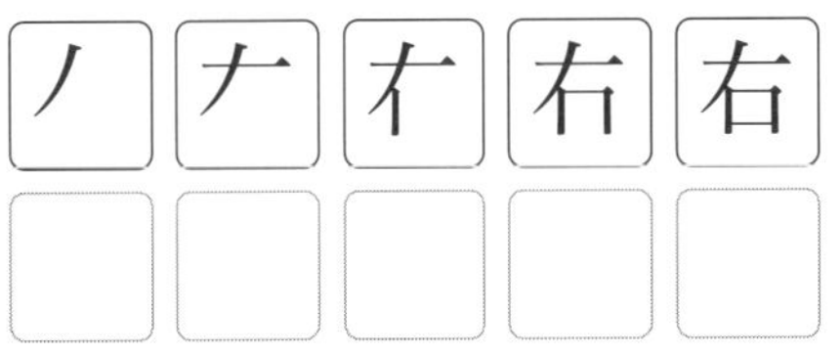

Boy: 右とひだりをまよったら...
If you're not sure which is left and which is right...

Boy: おはしをもつのがみぎて！おちゃわんがひだりて！
You hold chopsticks in your right hand! And the rice bowl in your left hand!

Girl: もっといいほうほうがあるだろ？
Isn't there a better way to remember?

COME

く(る)、ライ

ex. 来月 (らいげつ) - next month

ex. 来年 (らいねん) - next year

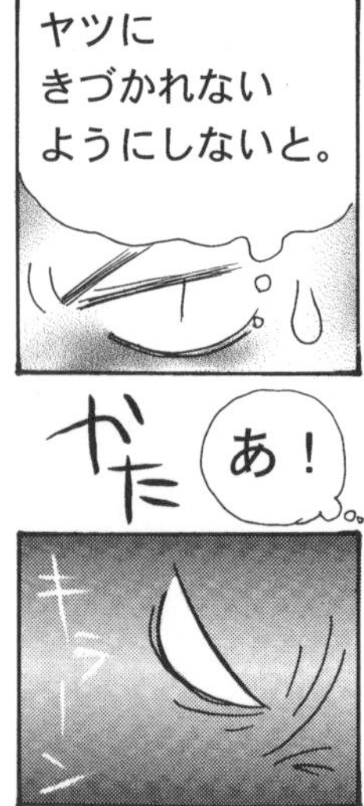

Mouse: ヤツにきづかれ
ないようにしないと。
I can't let him see me.

かた (strange noise)

あ！ Uh-oh!

キラーン (glint of cat's eye)

Mouse: 来たああああ
Here he comes!

GO

い(く)、おこな(う)、コウ、ギョウ

ex. 行く (いく) - to go

ex. 旅行* (りょこう) - travel

Mother: はいしゃに行くわよ。

We're going to the dentist.

Boy: うわーん、行きたくなーい！

Waaahh! I don't want to go!

ENTER / PUT IN

い(る)、い(れる)、はい(る)、ニュウ

ex. 入口* (いりぐち) - entrance
ex. 入学 (にゅうがく) - matriculation

Businessman: たかいビル だなぁ。
That sure is a tall building.

えーと… 入ぐちはこっちか。
Let's see...The entrance is this way.

入ぐち ("Entrance" sign)

LEAVE / TAKE OUT

で(る)、だ(す)、シュツ

ex. 出口* (でぐち) - exit

ex. 出前 (でまえ) - home-delivered food

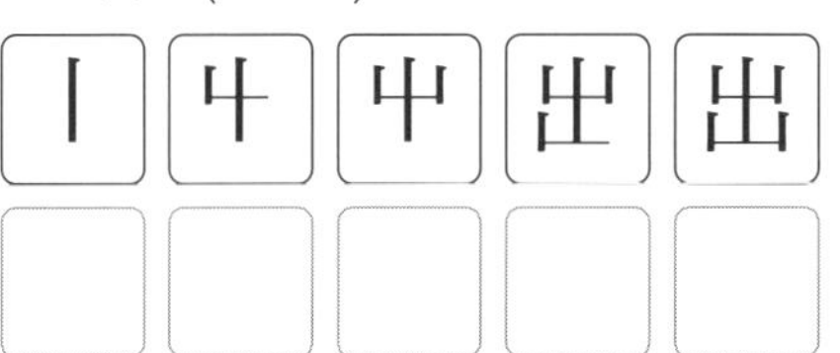

Frightened girl: このへんオバケが出そう…
I'm sure ghosts come out around here...

Frightened girl: 出たぁ！
They're on the loose!

キャー (breathless scream)
ちゅー (squeak of mouse)
ビクッ (sound of surprise)
ドキドキ (heavy heartbeats)

Ghost: 出るほうがおどろいたよ。にんげんこわい。
I'm supposed to do the haunting, but humans scare me!

REST

やす(む)、やす(まる)、キュウ

ex. 夏休み (なつやすみ) - summer vacation
ex. 休日 (きゅうじつ) - holiday; day off

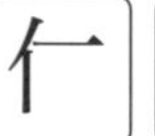

はあ はあ
(heavy panting)

ぜーはー
(slower panting)

Hiker: ちょっと休けい。
Time to rest.

OUTSIDE

そと、ほか、はず(す)、ガイ

ex. 外国人 (がいこくじん) - foreigner
ex. 外食 (がいしょく) - eating out

Mother: たまには外でうんどうしなさい！
You need to go outside and get some exercise!

Boy: え...　さむいんだもん...
(Whining) But it's so cold...

SMALL

ちい(さい)、こ、お、ショウ

ex. 小雨 (こさめ) - light rain (drizzle)
ex. 小学校 (しょうがっこう) - primary school

Girl: わぁ… 小さくて… かわいい！
Ah... How small...And adorable!

お…お…
おおきくても
かわいいよ。
Oh, of course, the big ones are cute too.

MIDDLE / IN

なか、チュウ

ex. 中学校 (ちゅうがっこう) - middle school
ex. 中国 (ちゅうごく) - China

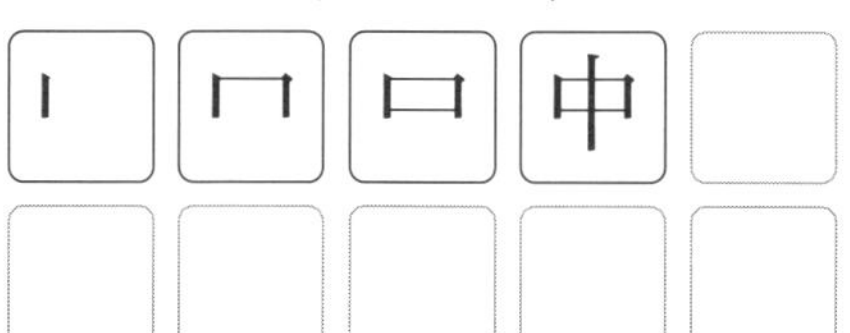

Boy: このハコの中って
なにかな？
I wonder what's in this box?

わーっ！
Yikes!

ビヨヨヨ
(boing)

BIG

おお、おお(きい)、ダイ、タイ

ex. 大人 (おとな) - adult

ex. 大学 (だいがく) - university

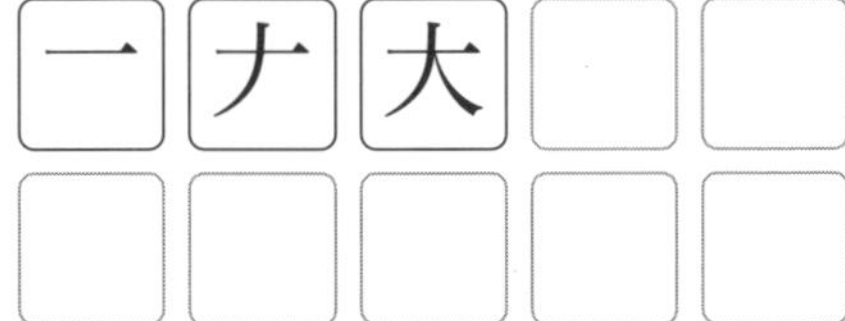

Mother: おにぎりたべる？
Do you want to eat a rice ball?

Boy: うん。
Please!

Boy: 大きすぎ…
It's too big...

どーん
(sound of surprise, similar to "gong")

CHIEF / LONG

なが(い)、チョウ

ex. 校長 (こうちょう) - school principal
ex. 長男 (ちょうなん) - eldest son

Girl: マフラーあんだの。してみて。にあうといいんだけど。
I knitted a muffler. Try it on. I hope you like it.

Boy: わーい。
Thanks!

Boy: でもこれ、長すぎない？
But isn't it too long?

Girl: こうするのよ。
This is how we wear it.

MAN

おとこ、ダン、ナン

ex. 男の人 (おとこのひと) - man
ex. 男の子 (おとこのこ) - boy

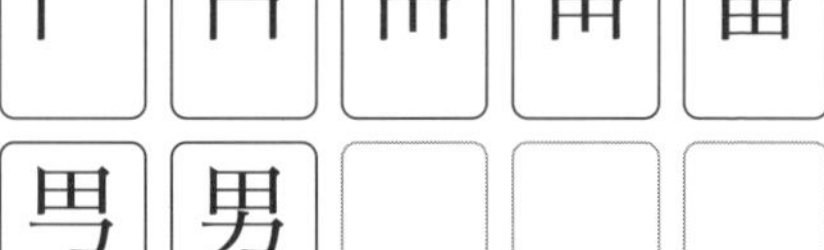

Girl: 男なんだから、なんとかしなさいよ！
You're a boy, do something!

Boy: そんなこといったって…
Yeah, but...

Boy: こわいものはこわいんだよー！わー！
He's so scary! Yikes!

ガルルル
(dog's growl)

WOMAN

おんな、ジョ

ex. 女の人 (おんなのひと) - woman
ex. 女の子 (おんなのこ) - girl

Boy: おもいにもつはもつよ。
I'll carry the heavy ones!

Girl: 女だからって、
Just because I'm a girl...

つん (humph)

Girl: あまくみないで！
...doesn't mean I'm weak and helpless!

フンッ (oomph)

パチパチパチ (clapping)

FATHER

ちち、フ

ex. お父さん (おとうさん) - father (polite)
ex. 父母 (ふぼ) - parents

Teacher: さくぶんはかいたかな？
Did everyone finish their essays?

Students (in unison): はーい Yes!

Boy (reading essay): ぼくは、しょうらい お父さんのように... "My Father": When I grow up...

Father (listening): なりたいとか？！He wants to be like me?!

ふけいさんかん(び) ("Parents Day" sign)

Boy (still reading): ふとらないように うんどうをします！
I'll exercise so I won't be fat like him!

MOTHER

はは、ボ

ex. お母さん (おかあさん) - mother (polite)
ex. 母国語 (ぼこくご) - mother tongue

Boy: お母さんのりょうりがいちばん！
おかわりー。
Mom, your cooking is the best!
Some more, please!

Mother: ありがとう。
どんどんたべてね.
Thank you! Eat up!

PERSON

ひと、ジン、ニン

ex. 一人 (ひとり) - one person; alone
ex. 日本人 (にほんじん) - Japanese (people)

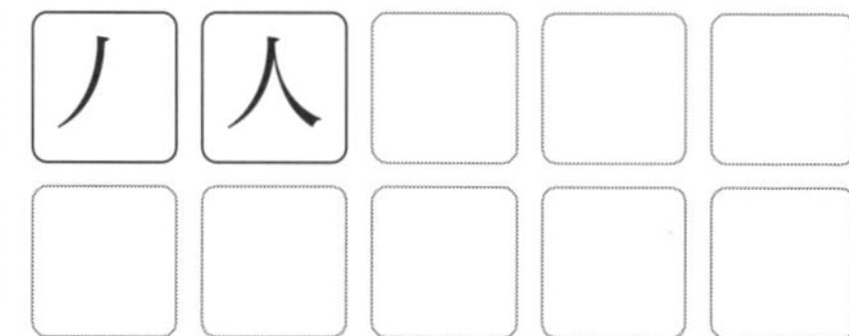

First boy: きゅうじつにもなると…
Come the weekend...

Second boy: どこもかしこも…
No matter which way you turn...

Both boys: 人ばっかり！
People are everywhere!

CHILD

こ、ご、シ、ス

ex. 子供たち* (こどもたち) - children
ex. 子守* (こもり) - babysitter

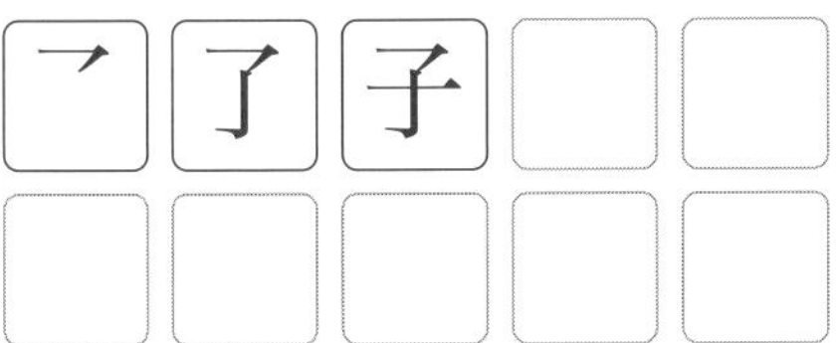

Toddler: えーん　えーん
わーん うわーん うえーん わーんん
(crying sounds)
おかあさーん…
Mommy!

Boy: まい子かなぁ…
A lost child?

FRIEND

とも、ユウ

ex. 友だち (ともだち) - friend(s)
ex. 学友 (がくゆう) - classmate

Children (in unison): 友だち！
Friends!

LIFE / RAW

い(きる)、う(まれる)、セイ、ショウ

ex. 生まれる (うまれる) - to be born
ex. 人生 (じんせい) - life

    生

Sister: シチューつくったの。たべて。
I made stew. Eat up!

Brother: いただきます！
Thanks!

ガリ (sound of shock)

Brother: ジャガイモがまだ生だよー。
The potato is still raw!

Sister: ごめーん。
Sorry.

MOUNTAIN

やま、サン

ex. 富士山* (ふじさん) - Mt. Fuji
ex. 火山 (かざん) - volcano

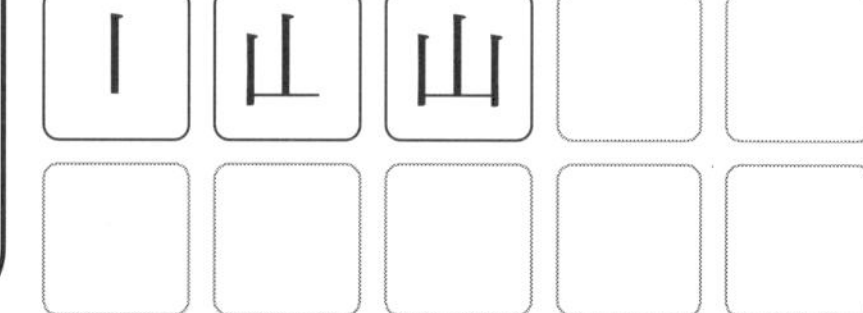

Girl: 山のぼりしたいなぁ。
I'd love to go mountain-climbing.

やっほー！
(Sound of yodeling)

山びこききたいな。
Then I can hear the echo of my voice in the mountains!

RIVER

かわ、がわ、セン

ex. 小川 (おがわ) - small river (stream)

ex. 川下 (かわしも) - downstream

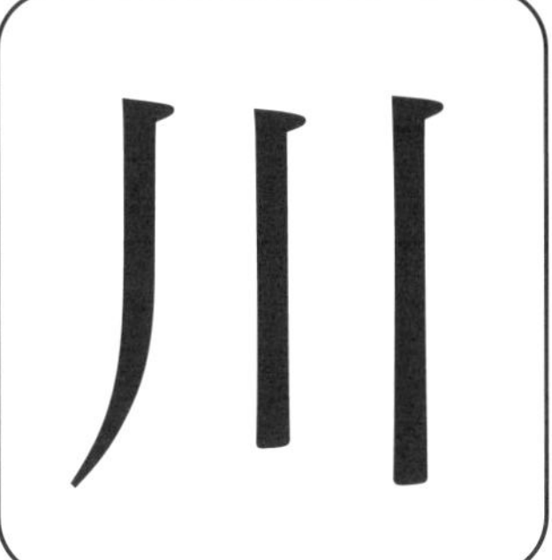

Mother: 川のじになってねてる。
They're sleeping side-by-side.

In Japan, it is common for children and parents to sleep together. When three family members (usually the mother one on side, father on the other and a small child in the middle, are lying next to one another, the formation resembles the kanji character for river (川) and is thus called a kawa-no-ji ("kanji for river").

HEAVEN / SKY

あま、あめ、テン

ex. 天気 (てんき) - weather

ex. 雨天 (うてん) - rainy weather

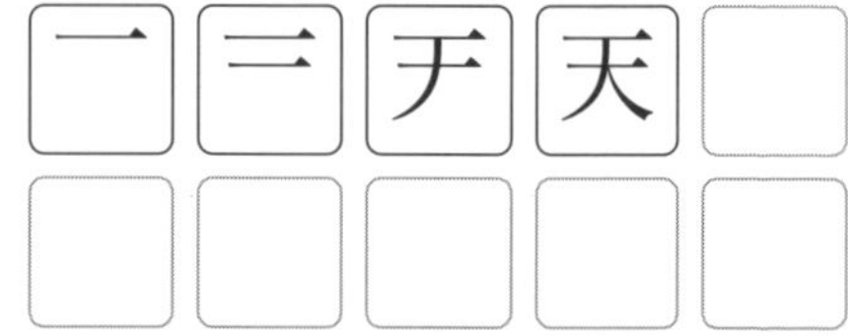

Girl: あかちゃんて、天しみたいにかわいいな。
Babies are as cute as angels!

きゃっ　きゃっ
(Sound of baby cooing)

Girl: いだだだだだだ！
Eeeooowww!

SPIRIT / GAS

キ、ケ

ex. 電気 (でんき) - electricity

ex. 気分 (きぶん) - feeling; mood

Mother: 行ってらっしゃい、気をつけてね。
See you later! Be careful now!

Boy: いってきます。だいじょうぶ！
See ya. I'll be fine!

Boy: わっ。
Oops.

こけっ
(tripping noise)

Mother: (speechless)

RAIN

あめ、あま、ウ

ex. 大雨 (おおあめ) - heavy rain
ex. 雨水 (あまみず) - rainwater

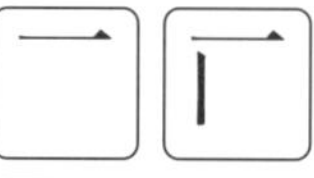

Girl: ん？雨？
Huh? Rain?

ポッ
(sound of a single drop of rain)

ザー
(sound of heavy rain)

Girl: (speechless)

WHITE

しろ、しら、しろ(い)、ハク

ex. 白鳥* (はくちょう) - swan

ex. 白人 (はくじん) - Caucasian

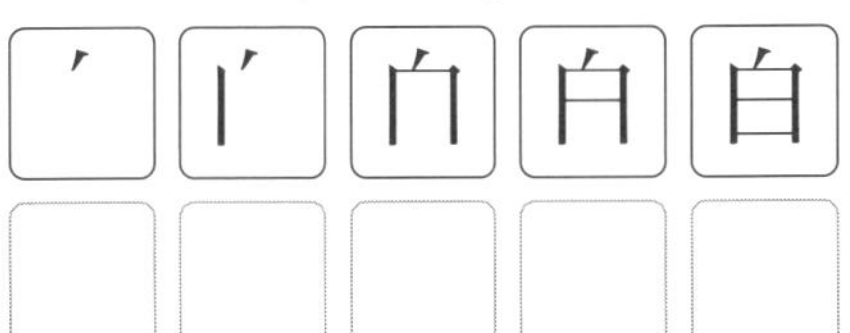

Boy: おかあさん、ごめんなさい。
Mom, I'm sorry.

Mother: どうしたの？
What's wrong?

Boy: 白いシャツよごしちゃった。
I got my white shirt dirty!

ガーン
(sound of realization)

ドロ　ドロ
(wet, muddy sound)

LEARN

まな(ぶ)、ガク

ex. 学生 (がくせい) - student
ex. 学年 (がくねん) - grade in school

Student: 学こうはたのしいけど…
School is a lot of fun, but...

Person in background: おはよう。
Good morning!

学ぶのはにがて。
Studying is a drag.

SCHOOL

コウ

ex. 学校 (がっこう) - school
ex. 校歌* (こうか) - school song

Principal: 校かせいしょう！
Let's sing our school song!

Student: 校ちょうせんせいっておんち！
The principal is totally tone deaf!

SEE

み(る)、み(える)、み(せる)、ケン

ex. 見本 (みほん) - sample
ex. 見学 (けんがく) - field trip

丨	冂	冃	月	目
貝	見			

Girls (in unison after seeing UFO): いまの見た？
Did you see that?

Girl on left: 見たわ。
I saw it.

Girl on left: わたしも。
Me too.

HEAR

き(く)、き(こえる)、ブン

ex. 新聞* (しんぶん) - newspaper

ex. 聞き手* (ききて) - listener; audience

ex. 見聞 (けんぶん) - knowledge; information

うと うと
(sound of boy nodding off to sleep)

ピキッ
(sound of teacher noticing boy)

Teacher: そこぉぉぉ、聞いとるのかぁぁぁぁ！
Are you listening to me?!

スコーン
(sound of boy being hit by teacher's pointer)

SPEAK / TALK

はな(す)、はなし、ワ

ex. 話 (はなし) - story, speech
ex. 電話* (でんわ) - telephone
ex. 会話* (かいわ) - conversation

Student: あーあ。
げつようびは
ゆううつだなぁ。
Sigh...Monday's are such a drag.

こうちょうせんせいの話がながすぎなんだよー。
I swear the principal talks too much.

LANGUAGE

かた(る)、かた(らう)、ゴ

ex. 日本語 (にほんご) - Japanese language
ex. 英語* (えいご) - English language
ex. 語学 (ごがく) - linguistics

Girl: べんきょうなんかしてどうしたの？めずらしいわね。
You're actually studying? What's up with that?

Boy: あした、にほん語のかんじテストなんだ。
I have a kanji test in my Japanese-language class tomorrow.

Girl: どうりでね。
That explains it.

READ

よ(む)、トウ、トク、ドク

ex. 読者 (どくしゃ) - reading book
ex. 音読み* (おんよみ) - on-reading (of kanji)
ex. 訓読み* (くんよみ) - kun-reading (of kanji)

Girl: いま、わだいの しょうせつか。
So, this is that popular new novel.

おもしろそう！読んでみようっと。
Looks interesting. I'm gonna read it!

WRITE

か(く)、ショ

ex. 書道* (しょどう) - calligraphy

ex. 書店* (しょてん) - bookstore

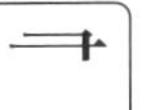

Boy: 書けたぞ！

I've written my masterpiece!

でりゃあああ

(Sound of furious writing)

EAT / FOOD

た(べる)、く(う)、ショク

ex. 食べ物* (たべもの) - food
ex. 食事* (しょくじ) - meal

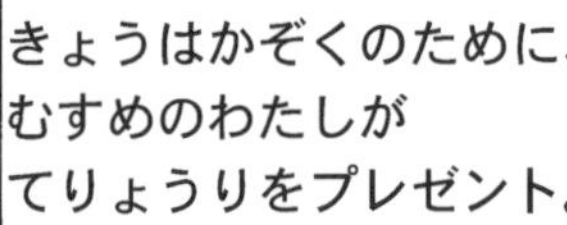

Girl: きょうは かぞくの ために、むすめのわたしが てりょうりをプレゼント。
Tonight, I, the loving daughter, shall make dinner for my family.

Family (thinking alike): 食べられる のか？りょうり？！
Will we be able to eat it?!

BOOK / MAIN

もと、ホン

ex. 絵本* (えほん) - picture book

ex. 日本 (にほん) - Japan

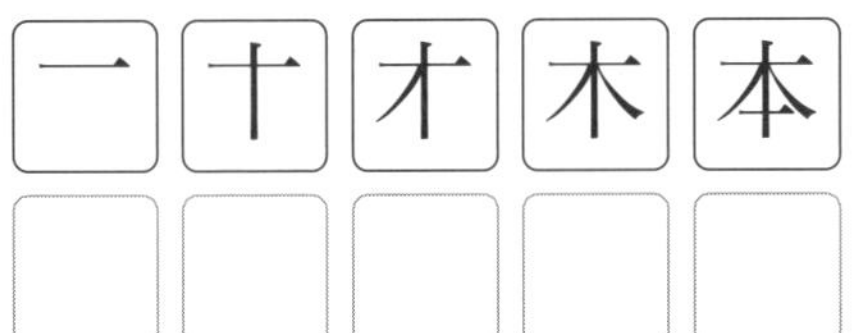

Schoolboy: 本つみすぎちゃった。
I've piled the books too high.

ぐらぐら (sound of shaking objects)

ドサ ドサ ドサ
(sound of falling objects)

トホホ...
Whimper...

ELECTRICITY

デン

ex. 電子 (でんし) - electronic
ex. 電子メール (でんしメール) - e-mail
ex. 電池* (でんち) - battery

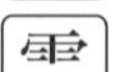

Girl: わー！てい電。かいちゅう電とうは？
Yikes! A blackout.
Where's the flashlight?

パッ
(shining light)

Boy (in scary voice): こーこーにあーるーよー。
Heeeere it is.

Girl: キャー
Eeeek.

ポウ…
(shining light)

VEHICLE / WHEEL

くるま、シャ

ex. 車 (くるま) - car
ex. 電車 (でんしゃ) - train

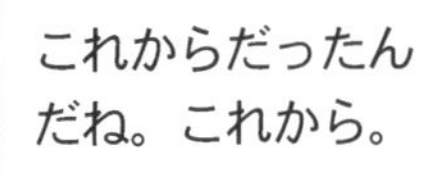

Boy: じどう車めんきょとったぞー！
I just got my driver's license!

Girl: じどう車は？
You have a car?

ザグッ
(sound of sudden realization)

Boy: ない。
...no car...

Girl: これからだったんだね。これから。すぐにかえるよ。
One step at a time. You'll be able to buy one soon.

NAME

な、メイ、ミョウ

ex. 名前 (なまえ) - name
ex. 名刺* (めいし) - business card

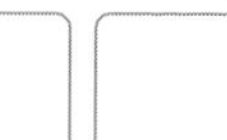

Teacher: つぎのひと名まえをよびます。
○○○くん。
I'm going to read the next person's name.
Mr._ _ _.

Boy: (answering before his name is called): はいっ！
Here!

The use of circles (as above) is common in Japanese manga, and is equivalent to the use of underlines in English to mean "fill in the blanks."

COUNTRY

くに、コク

ex. 外国 (がいこく) - foreign country

ex. 入国 (にゅうこく) - entering a country

Boy: 国ってたくさんあるね。
There sure are a lot of different countries!

Girl: ねー。
Yep.

TAKE THE TEST!

The Japanese Language Proficiency Test has been held annually throughout the world since 1984. Administered by the Japanese government and the nonprofit Japan Foundation, the test evaluates and certifies the proficiency of non-native speakers of Japanese. There are four levels to the examination: Level 4 for beginners, Level 3 for intermediate students, Level 2 for those who are functionally literate in Japanese, and Level 1 for experts.

This book includes all 80 kanji students need to know to pass Level 4 of the JLPT. Subsequent volumes in the "Kanji de Manga" series will help students prepare for the higher levels.

For more information about the Japanese Language Proficiency Test, including examination locations in your country, please visit the Japan Foundation's "JLPT Communications Square" website at http://momo.jpf.go.jp/jlpt/e/about_e.html.

PRACTICE SECTION

KANJI INDEX

The 80 kanji featured in this volume of *Kanji de Manga* are indexed here based on their *on-yomi* and *kun-yomi* readings. This makes it easy to look up any kanji for which you know a pronunciation but cannot remember how the character is written. Because most kanji have more than one reading, you will find those characters listed multiple times in this index.

GLENN KARDY is the editor of several volumes in the renowned *How to Draw Manga* series of art-instruction guides, including *Getting Started*, the first book of its kind to be used at major universities in both the United States (UCLA) and Japan (Waseda). Glenn lives in the Tokyo suburb of Kawaguchi City with his wife, their daughter and a collection of Oakland A's bobblehead dolls.

CHIHIRO HATTORI, niece of legendary manga artist Eiichi Fukui, was a graphics designer at Tokyo-based TechnoArt before turning her attention full-time to her manga career. Chihiro and her husband live in Yokohama, where they enjoy fine food, fast cars and high fashion.

Front cover illustration by You Garmendia Ayala
Back cover illustration by Chihiro Hattori
Back cover CG color by Honepanda
Project coordinator: Kanako Umehara
Translator: Kahori Hirano
Copy editor: Mari Oyama

Special thanks to Edward Mazza

MANGA UNIVERSITY presents...

The Comic Book That Teaches You How To Read And Write Japanese!

Japanime

TOKYO SAN FRANCISCO

Manga University presents ... Kanji de Manga
The Comic Book That Teaches You
How To Read And Write Japanese!
Volume Two

ISBN 4-921205-03-5

Published by Japanime Co. Ltd.
3-31-18 Nishi-Kawaguchi
Kawaguchi-shi, Saitama 332-0021
Japan

First edition March 2005
Second edition October 2005

Printed in Japan

The Manga University Mission Statement

The mission of Manga University is to enlighten and educate the international community on all aspects of Japanese culture through the creative use of traditional manga artwork.

The university recognizes that manga transcends mainstream entertainment and possesses a unique ability to convey the true spirit of Japan, making the art form an ideal communicative tool to touch the lives and inspire the minds of Japan enthusiasts worldwide.

Our mission and philosophy are firmly rooted in the principles and conviction of the Japanese educational tradition and in the best ideals of Japanese heritage.

Founded at the turn of the century and located in Tokyo, Manga University is one of the world's foremost publishers of manga-themed educational materials.

CONTENTS

INTRODUCTION

Welcome to the second volume of *Kanji de Manga*, your guide to the exciting world of Japanese writing.

If you're reading this book, you probably already know the first 80 basic Japanese kanji characters. Maybe you learned them by studying the first book in our *Kanji de Manga* series. Perhaps you picked them up on a trip to Japan. Or maybe you studied some Japanese in school.

No matter how you learned them, give yourself a pat on the back—you're well on your way to learning the most difficult part of the Japanese language. And now you're ready for a new and stimulating challenge as you continue your journey.

By now, you've probably figured out a few things. First, that all those warnings were true: learning kanji is truly challenging. But at the same time, we hope you've found that it's not as difficult as you feared it might be—and that it really can be fun to learn Japanese through manga.

Secondly, you've probably already seen how far those 80 basic kanji can take you. Maybe for the first time you saw a sign in Japanese and instantly knew what it meant. Or perhaps you were able to read parts of a Japanese comic book.

And finally, you're probably starting to see how some of the basic strokes reappear in many different characters, and learning these strokes already has taken some of the mystery out of Japanese writing.

Now you're ready for the next step. And while it's still going to be challenging, it's going to be even more rewarding because in the end, you'll know twice as many characters!

In this book, we'll teach you 80 of the kanji that are needed to pass the third level of the Japanese Language Proficiency Test. (For more information about the test, please see page 92.) In Japan, these characters are taught between the first and fourth grades of grammar school.

Combined with the 80 characters you've already learned from the first volume (you *have* learned them by now, right?), the 160 kanji that will be part of your life when you reach the end of this book will take you deep into the world of Japanese writing.

And when you're ready for the next step, the next edition of *Kanji de Manga* will be there to help you through it.

So get those pens ready… *Gambatte!*

PAGE GUIDE

① The featured kanji

② Common definition

③ Readings: kun-yomi (Japanese readings) are written in hiragana, while on-yomi (Chinese readings) are in katakana.

④ Examples of compounds containing the featured kanji, their pronunciations (written in hiragana) and English definitions. (An asterisk next to a compound indicates that one or more of its kanji are not featured in this or the first volume of the "Kanji de Manga" series.)

⑤ Stroke order: In general, the strokes are written from top to bottom and left to right. For a list of additional stroke-order rules, please refer to the chart at the back of this book.

⑥ The manga. All dialogue is written in hiragana and katakana except for the single featured kanji. The proper pronunciation of the kanji is indicated in furigana (tiny hiragana) written above the character.

⑦ Translation of the dialogue and selected onomatopoeia.

STUDY SECTION

MEET / SOCIETY

あ(う)、カイ

ex. 会社 (かいしゃ) - company
ex. 社会 (しゃかい) - society
ex. 会話 (かいわ) - conversation

Girls (together): あれ？
Huh?

Girl on left: うわー！ひさしぶり。げんきだった？
Wow! Long time, no see. How have you been?

Girl on right: こんなところで会うなんておどろいたわ!
I'm so surprised to meet you here!

BLUE

あお、あお(い)、セイ

ex. 青空 (あおぞら) - blue sky
ex. 青天 (せいてん) - fine weather
ex. 青い鳥 (あおいとり) - bluebird

Astronaut: ちきゅうってほんとうに青いんだ！
The earth really is blue!

RED

ex. 赤十字 (せきじゅうじ) - The Red Cross
ex. 赤ちゃん (あかちゃん) - baby
ex. 赤字 (あかじ) - deficit ("in the red")

Boy (unseen): ただいま。
I'm home.

バタン… (sound of door closing)

Mother: おかえり。
そとはかなりさむかったみたいね。
Welcome back. It must be really cold out today.

Mother: ほっぺもはなも、みみまで赤いわよ。
Your cheeks, your nose and even your ears are red.

BRIGHT / CLEAR

あか(るい)、あき(らか)、メイ、ミョウ

ex. 明日 (あした) - tomorrow
ex. 明月 (めいげつ) - full (bright) moon
ex. 文明 (ぶんめい) - civilization

Girl: どうか、明すのぶんかさいは、はれますように！
Please let it be sunny for tomorrow's Culture Festival!

ぜったい、明すのぶんかさいは、はれてほしい！
Pleeeaaassseee let it be sunny for tomorrow's Culture Festival!

てるてるぼうずおねがい。どうかはれますように。
Teruterubozu,* please let it be sunny.

*A teruterubozu is a paper doll to which Japanese children pray for good weather.

AUTUMN

あき、シュウ

ex. 秋口 (あきぐち) - beginning of autumn
ex. 秋分 (しゅうぶん) - autumn equinox
ex. 秋風 (あきかぜ) - autumn wind

Girl: ふう… (sigh)

Boy: どうしたんだろう… ためいきなんか ついて…
What's up...
Why the long face...

Boy: 秋はやっぱりものがなしく なるのかなぁ…
Autumn does make one feel melancholy...

うんうん Yes, yes...

ロマンチックだもんな。
It's a romantic time.

Girl: おなか すいた…
I'm hungry...

はぁぁ (sigh)

Boy: かんどう！
I'm impressed!

MORNING

あさ、チョウ

ex. 今朝 (けさ) - this morning
ex. 明朝 (みょうちょう) - tomorrow morning
ex. 朝食 (ちょうしょく) - breakfast

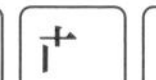

Schoolgirl: どうしたの？ 朝からちょうしわるそうよ。
What's wrong? You've seemed sick since the morning.

Schoolboy: まあね… Yeah...

ふあ〜… (yawn)

Schoolboy: じつは朝までずっとほんをよんでいてあまりねていないんだ。
Actually, I was reading a book till morning and didn't sleep.

Schoolgirl: (speechless) がく (sound of shock)

Schoolboy: すいりものでさ。とまらないんだ、これが... It was a mystery. I couldn't put it down...

FOOT / LEG

あし、たり(る)、たる、ソク

ex. 足早 (あしばや) - quick-footed
ex. 足跡* (あしあと) - footprint
ex. 足袋* (たび) - Japanese-style socks

Mother: むむっ！
Hey!

ゆかにどろの足あと？！
Muddy footprints all over the floor?!

Mother: だぁれ？足のうらがよごれているのは！足をあらいなさい！
Who? Who is the one with the dirty feet?! Go wash your feet now!

ELDER BROTHER

あに、キョウ、ケイ

ex. 兄嫁* (あによめ) - elder brother's wife
ex. 兄弟 (きょうだい) - siblings
ex. 父兄 (ふけい) - parents; guardians

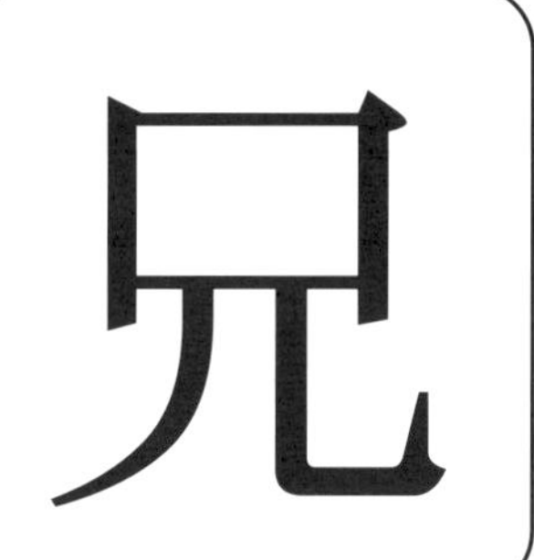

Mother: また
にんじんのこして！
You haven't eaten your carrots again!

Girl: だって、
きらいなんだもん。
Because I hate them.

Mother: お兄ちゃんのように
つよくなれないわよっ。
They'll make you strong like your big brother.

ムキムキ (sound of flexing muscles)

Girl: お兄ちゃんみたいになんかなりたくないよ！
But I don't want to be like him!

ELDER SISTER

あね、シ

ex. 姉妹 (しまい) - sisters
ex. お姉さん (おねえさん) - young lady
ex. 姉妹都市* (しまいとし) - sister cities

おぎゃーっ
おぎゃーっ (baby crying)

Nurse: ぼしともにけんこうな
おとこのこですよ。
Mother and baby are doing fine.

Nurse: おとうとだぞ。
きょうからお姉ちゃんだね。
It's a boy. Now you're a big sister.

Little girl: うん！
Yup!

Father: ほっ Whew...

WALK

ある(く)、あゆ(む)、ホ、ポ、ブ

ex. 歩道 (ほどう) - sidewalk; footpath
ex. 一歩一歩 (いっぽいっぽ) - step by step
ex. 歩兵* (ほへい) - foot soldier; infantryman

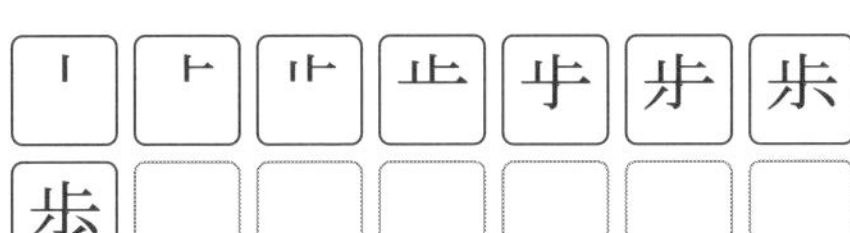

College student: ね、このあと こうえんでさん歩でもしない？
Hey, you wanna go for a stroll in the park?

Roommate: いいわね。
Good idea.

College student: みどりのなかを 歩くのってきもちいいよね。
It feels wonderful to walk outdoors.

Roommate: さん歩っていいわね。
Yeah, walks are great.

SAY / SPEECH

い(う)、こと、ゲン、ゴン

ex. 言語 (げんご) - language
ex. 言い合い* (いいあい) - quarrel; dispute
ex. 言葉* (ことば) - word(s); speech

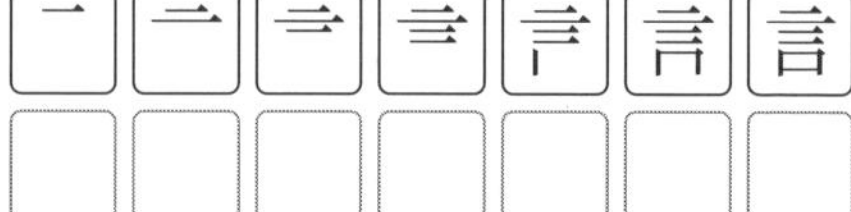

Schoolgirl: おとこらしくはっきりと言ったら？
Why don't you be a man and tell me what you want to say?

Schoolboy: …す
すっ……
(stuttering)

Schoolboy: すきだ
I like you!

ポッ (sound of surprise)

HOUSE / FAMILY

いえ、や、カ、ケ

ex. 家族* (かぞく) - family
ex. 家内* (かない) - household; wife
ex. 家計* (かけい) - housekeeping

Sister: え？！じぶんで家をたてたの？！
Huh?! You built a house all by yourself?!

Brother: 家っていっても、ポチの家だけど…
Well, yeah, a house, but just Pochi's doghouse...

Sister: すごいすごい！
Wow! Wonderful!

Dog: わんわんわん
Woof, woof

DOG

いぬ、ケン

ex. 犬小屋* (いぬごや) - doghouse; kennel
ex. 猟犬* (りょうけん) - hunting dog
ex. 犬かき (いぬかき) - dog paddle (swim)

一	ナ	大	犬			

Girl: 犬ってかわいいわね！
Dogs are so cute!

Girl: 犬ってかわいいとおもわない？
Don't you think dogs are cute?

Boy (frightened): そ…そうだね…
Sh... sure...

YOUNGER SISTER

いもうと、マイ

ex. 妹さん (いもうとさん) - younger sister
ex. 義妹* (いもうと) - younger sister-in-law
ex. 妹分 (いもうとぶん) - protogee

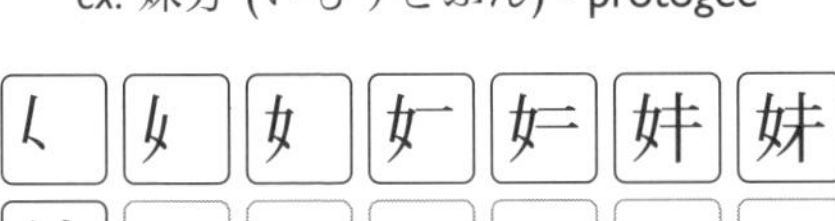

Girl: かわいい。
だれかにプレゼントするの?
How cute. Is it a present for someone?

Boy: うん。妹のたんじょうびプレゼント。
Yep. It's my younger sister's birthday present.

Girl: 妹おもいのおにいさんね。
You really care about your younger sister.

Boy: ありがとう。てれるなぁ。
Thanks. But now I'm embarrassed.

COLOR / PASSION

いろ、ショク、シキ

ex. 原色* (げんしょく) - primary colors
ex. 色彩* (しきさい) - hue; tint
ex. 顔色* (かおいろ) - complexion

Girl: わぁ！きれいな色の
おかしがたくさん！
Wow! There are so many
different-colored candies!

色とりどりだね。
A real variety of colors.

Girl: どうしよう…
色いろあって
めうつりしちゃう〜。
What should I do...
There are so many colors
to choose from.

FISH

うお、さかな、ギョ

ex. 金魚 (きんぎょ) - goldfish

ex. 魚座* (うおざ) - Pisces

ex. 人魚 (にんぎょ) - mermaid

Boy: ねぇ、おじさんて
魚やさんでしょ？！
Hey, mister, you work in a fish shop, don't you?!

Man: せいかい。なんで
わかったんだい？魚やだって。
That's right. How'd you know I worked in a fish shop?

Sign: 魚や (Fish Shop)

Boy: おじさんが魚みたいな
かおしているから!
Because your face looks like a fish!

ゲラゲラ (chuckling)
あははは (laughter)

CATTLE / COW

うし、ギュウ

ex. 牛肉 (ぎゅうにく) - beef
ex. 牛乳* (ぎゅうにゅう) - milk
ex. 子牛 (こうし) - calf

Boy: 牛がたくさんいるね。
There sure are a lot of cows.

ベロ
(sound of a tongue licking something)

Boy: (speechless)

SING / SONG

うた、うた(う)、カ

ex. 歌手 (かしゅ) - singer
ex. 歌を歌う (うたをうたう) - sing a song
ex. 国歌 (こっか) - national anthem

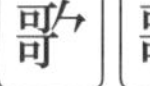

Schoolgirl: カラオケいこうよ！
Let's go to a karaoke club!

Friend: え？！いいよ、歌へただし。
Huh?! Forget it; I can't sing.

Classmates (thinking alike): ノリノリで歌ってるじゃない…しかもじょうずだし…
Look who's talking... She's a great singer...

SEA / BEACH

うみ、カイ

ex. 海外 (かいがい) - overseas; foreign
ex. 海辺* (うみべ) - seashore
ex. 海草* (かいそう) - seaweed

Boy: なつといえば...
Summer means...

海だー！
海！
海！
The sea!
Sea!
Sea!

SELL

う(る)、う(れる)、バイ

ex. 売店 (ばいてん) - shop; vendor's stall
ex. 安売り* (やすうり) - discount sale
ex. 発売中* (はつばいちゅう) - now on sale

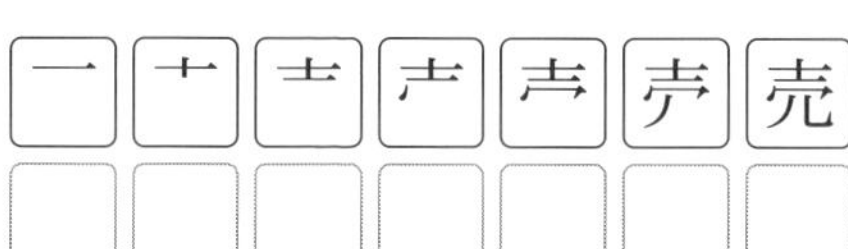

Big sister: ものがいっぱい だけど、いったいどうしたの？
You sure have out a lot of stuff. What's it for?

Little sister: こんどの フリーマーケットで 売りにだすものをせいりしていたの。
I'm looking for things to sell at the next flea market.

Big sister: たくさん売れるといいわね。
I hope you're able to sell a lot.

MANY

おお(い)、タ

ex. 多すぎる (おおすぎる) - too much
ex. 多忙* (たぼう) - very busy
ex. 多分 (たぶん) - probably

Boy on left: このへんてひとが多いね。
There's a lot of people around here.

Boy on right: 多いね。
Definitely a lot.

SOUND

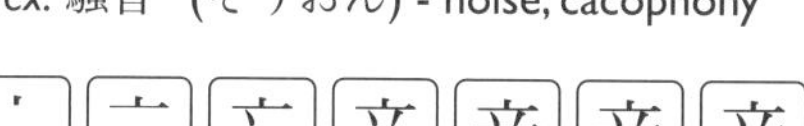

おと、ね、オン

ex. 音楽 (おんがく) - music
ex. 音声* (おんせい) - voice
ex. 騒音* (そうおん) - noise; cacophony

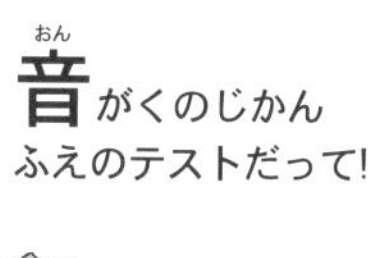

Girl: 音がくのじかんふえのテストだって！
There's going to be a test during music class!

Boy: れんしゅうしなくちゃ。
We've gotta practice.

ばっ (sound of book being opened)

びっしり (sound of abundance; the students are shocked when they look at the sheet music and realize how much they must practice)

ふらー (sound of fainting)

Girl: わあああ！しっかりして！
Hey! Get a grip!

YOUNGER BROTHER

おとうと、ダイ、テイ、デ

ex. 義弟* (おとうと) - younger brother-in-law
ex. 弟子 (でし) - disciple; apprentice
ex. 異父兄弟* (いふきょうだい) - half-brother

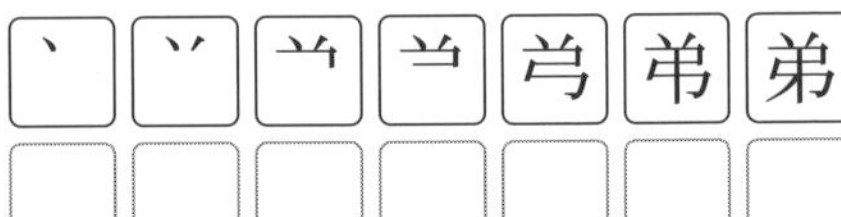

Teen-age boy: あれ？きみって弟がいたんだ。
Huh? I didn't know you had a younger brother.

Teen-age girl: そうなの。弟だってよくわかったね。
That's right. But how'd you know he's my brother?

Teen-age girl: ほら、あいさつして。
Say hello.

Little boy: こんにちは。Hello.

Teen-age boy: だって、そっくりだもん。こんにちは...
You two look so alike. Hello...

SAME

おな(じ)、ドウ

ex. 同日 (どうじつ) - the same day
ex. 同志* (どうし) - kindrid spirit; soulmate
ex. 同様* (どうよう) - similar

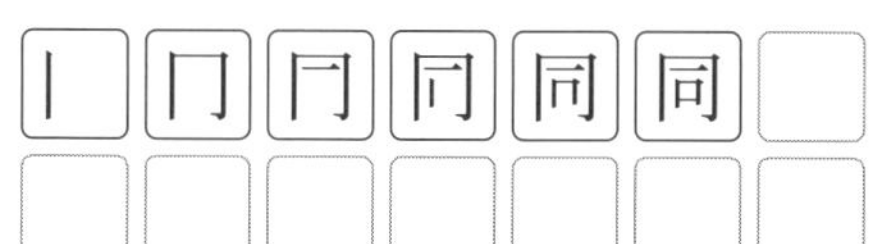

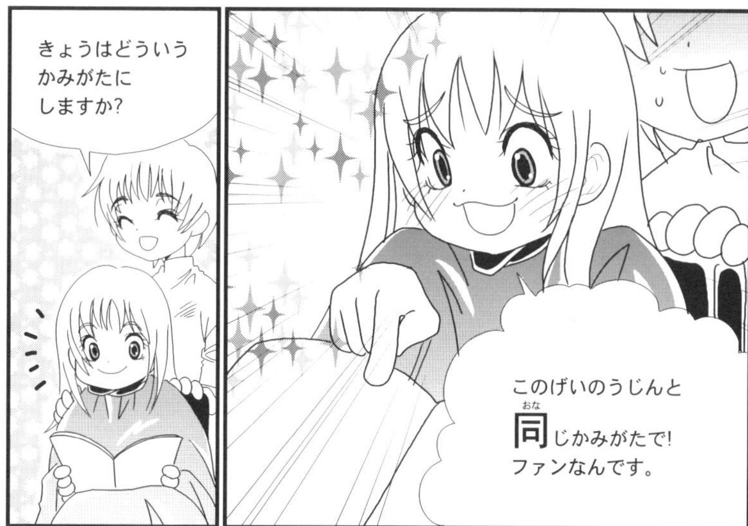

Beautician: きょうは
どういうかみがたに
しますか？
Have you decided
what kind of hairstyle
you want?

Customer: このげいのうじんと
同じかみがたで！
ファンなんです。
I want the same style as this
celebrity! I'm a big fan.

THINK

おも(う)、シ

ex. 思い出 (おもいで) - memories
ex. 不思議* (ふしぎ) - wonder; mystery
ex. 思想* (しそう) - thought; idea; ideology

Young woman: なつかしいな。 わぁ… How nostalgic. Wow…	いろいろな思いでが つまっていて… It's full of so many good memories.
アルバムだぁ。 My photo album.	じぶんのたからもの だと思うわ。 I think of it as my treasure.

PICTURE

ガ、カク

ex. 画家 (がか) - artist; painter
ex. 漫画* (まんが) - manga (cartoon; comic)
ex. 映画* (えいが) - movie

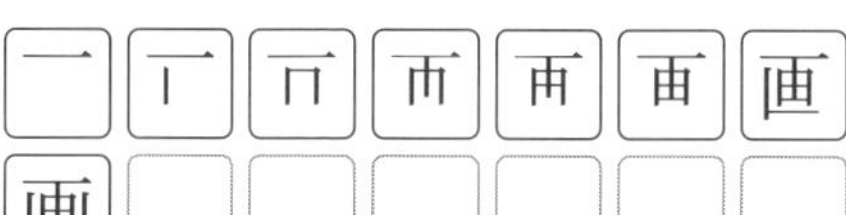

Sign: かい画てんじかい (Art Exhibition)

Visitor: さすが画はく！
You're a wonderful painter!

News reporter: 画はくひとこと。
Please tell us about your picture.

Boy (daydreaming):
なんちゃって...
Woudn't that be great...

BUY

か(う)、バイ

ex. 買い主* (かいぬし) - buyer
ex. 買い物* (かいもの) - shopping
ex. 買収* (ばいしゅう) - bribery

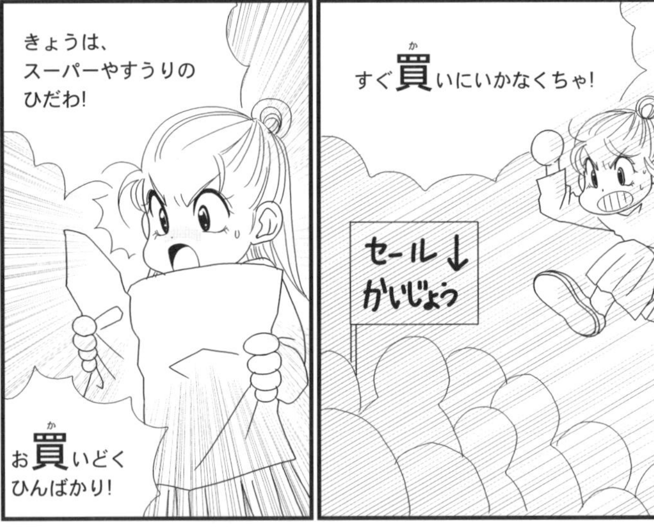

Housewife: きょうは、
スーパーやすうりの
ひだわ！
There's a special sale at the supermarket today!

お買いどくひんばかり！
Lots of good buys!

すぐ買いにいかなくちゃ！
I've gotta get there early to shop!

Sign: セールかいじょう (Sales Floor)

RETURN

かえ(る)、かえ(す)、キ

ex. 帰宅* (きたく) - returning home
ex. 帰国 (きこく) - returning to one's country
ex. 帰り道 (かえりみち) - the way back home

Boy (running): ただいまー！I'm home!
ドタドタ (sound of boy running up the stairs)
Mother: おかえり。...ちょっと！ちょっとまちなさい！
Hi. ...Hey! Hey, wait!
帰ったらくつくらいそろえなさい。
おやつぬきにするからね！
Put your shoes away when you return home or there will be no snacks for you!

Mother: (speechless)

Boy: (speechless)

いそいそ (sound of shoes being dragged across the floor)

WIND

かぜ、かざ、フウ

ex. 台風 (たいふう) - typhoon

ex. 風邪* (かぜ) - cold (illness)

ex. 風変わり* (ふうがわり) - strange

Wife: こんにちは。 Hey. *Husband:* 風がわりなかみがたしてなにかあった？ What's with the strange hairstyle?	*Wife:* そと、風がつよくてこんなになっちゃった。 The strong wind did this. ビュー (sound of a wind gust) *Husband:* おつかれ。 Poor you.

WAY OF DOING

かた、ホウ

ex. 作り方 (つくりかた) - the way to make
ex. 方言 (ほうげん) - dialect
ex. 正方形* (せいほうけい) - square

Big brother: どうしたの？こまっているみたい。
What's wrong? You look like you could use some help.

Little brother: じつは、すうがくのもんだいで、とき方がわからないもんだいがあるんだ。
I don't know how to do this math problem.

Big brother: あぁ、このもんだいはしたのこうしきをつかった方がいいよ。
Ah, with this type of problem, it's best to do it the way that's written here.

Little brother: ありがとう。これならとけそうだよ。
Thanks. I think I can solve it now.

PAPER

かみ、シ

ex. 折り紙* (おりがみ) - origami
ex. 紙袋* (かみぶくろ) - paper bag
ex. 包装紙* (ほうそうし) - wrapping paper

だい5かい
おり紙(がみ)てん

てんじ みて みない?

いいよ。

すべており紙(がみ)で できているなんて しんじられない!

おり紙(がみ)って すごいのね。 しらなかったわ。

Sign: だい５かい
おり紙てん
(5th Origami Exhibition)

First girl: てんじみてみない？
You want to check out the exhibition?

Second girl: いいよ。 Sure.

First girl: すべており紙で
できているなんてしんじられない！
I can't believe all the things that are made with origami!

Second girl: おり紙ってすごいのね。
しらなかったわ。
Origami really is amazing. I never knew.

THINK

かんが(える)、コウ

ex. 考え事* (かんがえごと) - deep thinking

ex. 考査* (こうさ) - examination; test

ex. 考案* (こうあん) - idea; plan

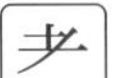

Schoolboy: うーん
Hmm...

うーんと…
Uhhh...

考えても
考えても
ぜんぜんわからないよ！
I think...
and I think...
and still I can't understand any of this!

CAPITAL

キョウ、ケイ

ex. 東京 (とうきょう) - Tokyo
ex. 京都* (きょうと) - Kyoto
ex. 北京 (ぺきん) - Beijing

College student: じょう京してはや3ねん…
It's been 3 years since I've been to the capital city...

よし！
All right!

ビシッ ("sound" of looking good)

スーツきるのも
さまになってきたかな。
I feel like I finally belong in this suit!

CUT

きる、きっ、セツ、サイ

ex. 大切 (たいせつ) - important; valuable
ex. 切手 (きって) - postage stamp
ex. 切符* (きっぷ) - ticket

Housewife (singing to herself):
おりょうり。おりょうり。
Cooking. Cooking.

トントントントントントン
(chopping sound)

ゆび切ったぁぁぁぁぁぁぁぁぁ！
I cut my fingerrrrrrrrrrrrr!

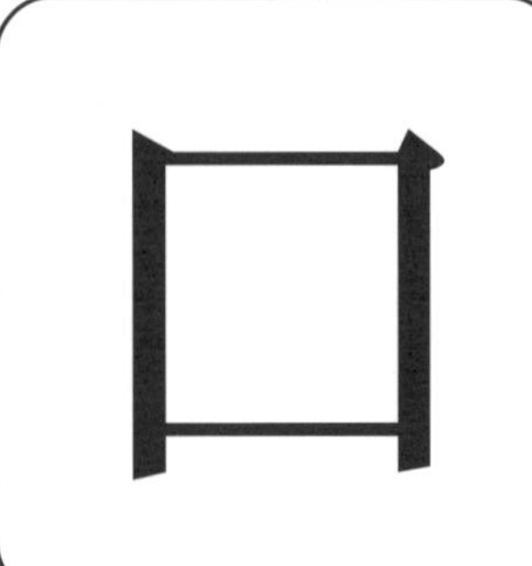

MOUTH

くち、コウ、ク

ex. 口拭き* (くちふき) - napkin
ex. 口づけ (くちづけ) - kiss
ex. 口笛* (くちぶえ) - whistle

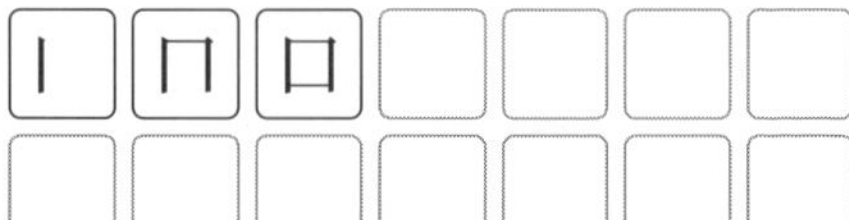

Sister: さっき、ごはん たべた？
Did you just finish eating?

Brother: なっ、なんでそんな ことわかるの？
Yeah, how did you know?

Sister: だって、口のまわりに ごはんがついてるから。
Because you've got rice stuck around your mouth.

BLACK

くろ、くろ(い)、コク

ex. 黒猫* (くろねこ) - black cat
ex. 黒人 (こくじん) - black person
ex. 黒帯* (くろおび) - black belt (martial arts)

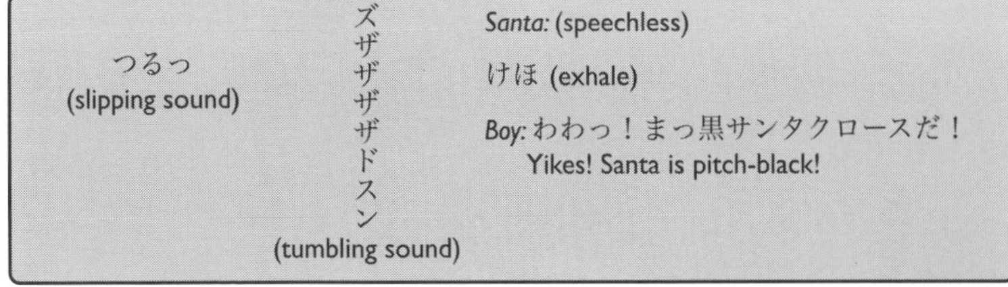

つるっ
(slipping sound)

ズザザザドスン
(tumbling sound)

Santa: (speechless)

けほ (exhale)

Boy: わわっ！まっ黒サンタクロースだ！
Yikes! Santa is pitch-black!

MANUFACTURE

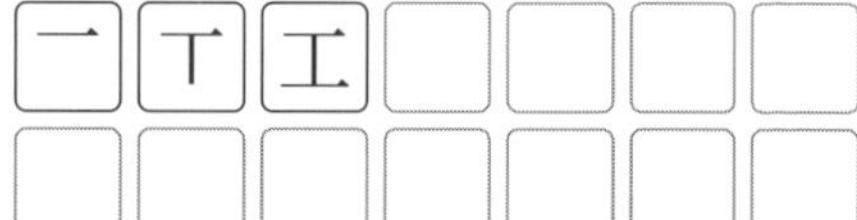

コウ、ク

ex. 工事* (こうじ) - construction work
ex. 工場* (こうじょう) - factory
ex. 人工 (じんこう) - man-made

First boy: 工じょうがたくさんあるとくうきがわるいね。
All of these factories sure make the air bad around here.

Second boy: うん。
Yup.

HEART / SPIRIT

こころ、シン

ex. 心細い* (こころぼそい) - lonely
ex. 心音 (しんおん) - heartbeat (sound of)
ex. 心残り* (こころのこり) - regret

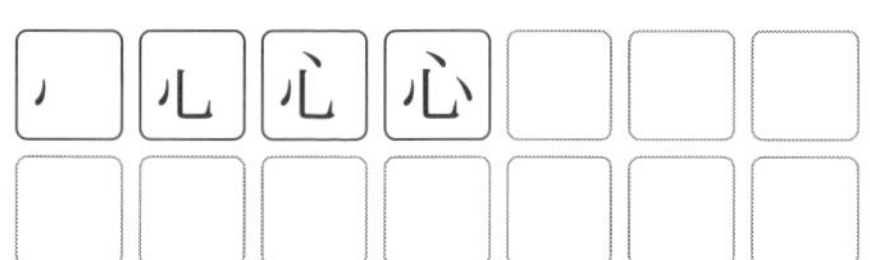

Sister: あしたからみなみのしまに りょこう…
Tomorrow we begin vacationing on a southern island…
ほわんほわん (happiness in the heart)
心がはずむわぁ。
My heart is beating with excitement.

Brother: 心ここにあらずだな…
Her heart is already in another place…

ANSWER / REPLY

こた(え)、こた(える)、トウ

ex. 答える (こたえる) - to reply
ex. 答案用紙* (とうあんようし) - exam paper
ex. 解答* (かいとう) - answer; solution

ノ	⺈	⺮	𠂉	⺮	竺	笑
笑	笁	笞	答	答		

Teacher: このもんだいの答えがわかるひとはいるかな？
Does anyone know the answer to the question?

Students (in unison): はーい
Ye-essss!

CHARACTER

ジ

ex. 漢字* (かんじ) - kanji
ex. 字画 (じかく) - kanji stroke count
ex. 字体* (じたい) - font; lettering

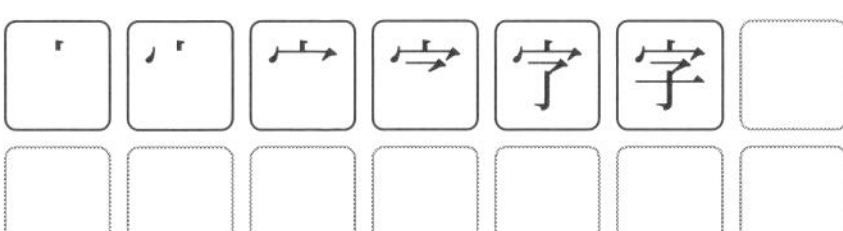

Schoolboy: うわっ。
きたない字だな。
Wow. What messy writing.

なんてかいてあるのか
まったくよめないよ...
I can't read this at all...

WEEK

シュウ

ex. 先週 (せんしゅう) - last week
ex. 今週 (こんしゅう) - this week
ex. 週末* (しゅうまつ) - weekend

キュッ (sound of pencil on paper)	*Boy:* あしたはげつようび… 1週かんってたつのがはやいなぁ。 Tomorrow's Monday...The week sure goes by quickly. しみじみ (sound of confidence)
	Mother: はやくねなさい。もう、おそいわよ。 Hurry up and go to bed. It's already late.

KNOW

し(る)、チ

ex. 知能* (ちのう) - intelligence
ex. 知人 (ちじん) - acquaintance
ex. 知識* (ちしき) - knowledge

Teacher: このかんじのよみかた知ってる？
Do you know how to read this kanji?

Student: ああ、これはこう。
Ah, like this.

Teacher: これは？
This one?

Student: こっちのよみかた。
It's read like this.

Teacher: あとこれ。
And this?

Student: これはこう。
This way.

Teacher: すごくかんじのよみかた知ってるんだね。いやぁ、てれるよ。
You know how to read a lot of kanji. I'm impressed.

Student: さすが。
It's nothing.

LITTLE

すく(ない)、すこ(し)、ショウ

ex. 少しずつ (すこしずつ) - little by little
ex. 少女 (しょうじょ) - little (young) girl
ex. 少年 (しょうねん) - little (young) boy

Schoolboy: ふー…
Whew...

あと少しで…
Just a little more...

しゅくだいがおわりそう!
And my homework will be done!

SKY / AIR / EMPTY

そら、あ(く)、あ(ける)、から、クウ

ex. 空色 (そらいろ) - sky-blue
ex. 空港* (くうこう) - airport
ex. 空手 (からて) - karate (empty hands)

Boy: 空はあおくてきれいだし。
The sky is so blue and beautiful.

空きはおいしいし。
The air smells so fresh.

しぜんって
さいこうだなぁ。
Nature is wonderful.

RICE FIELD

た、デン

ex. 田んぼ (たんぼ) - farmland; rice paddy
ex. 田植え* (たうえ) - rice planting
ex. 田園* (でんえん) - rural area

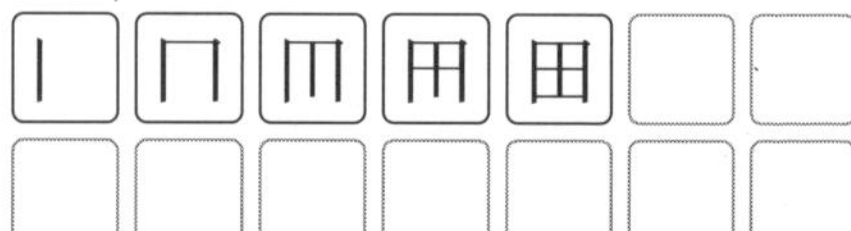

Father: 田んぼにおたまじゃくし。
There are tadpoles in this paddy field.

Son: たくさん。
Lots of 'em.

Father: おとうさんがこどものころは このへんは田んぼだらけだったんだよ。
When daddy was your age, there were a lot more rice paddies around here.

Daughter: そうなんだ。 Is that so?

Son: へぇー Really?

STANDAND / TABLE

ダイ、タイ

ex. 台紙 (だいし) - cardboard
ex. 台所* (だいどころ) - kitchen
ex. 台湾* (たいわん) - Taiwan

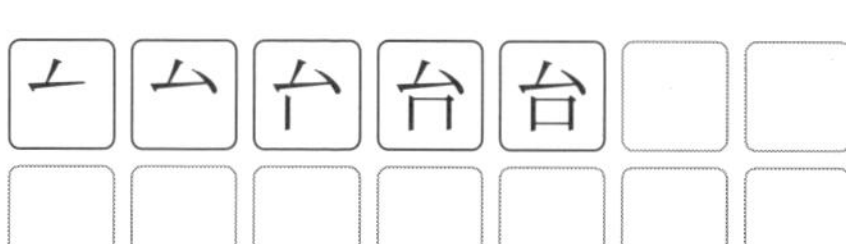

Girl (reaching): あと
もうすこし…
Just a bit more...

なにか台になるものないかなぁ。
I wonder if there's a stand I can use.

台になるもの。
Something like a stool.

CORRECT

ただ(しい)、ただ(す)、セイ、ショウ

ex. 正解* (せいかい) - correct answer
ex. 正誤* (せいご) - correction
ex. 正月 (しょうがつ) - New Year

Teacher: もんだいです。
Here's the question.
正しいものは
どれでしょう?
Which is the correct answer?

Student: いち!
Number one!

Teacher: 正かい!
Correct!

STAND

た(つ)、た(てる)、リツ

ex. 立ち席* (たちせき) - standing room only
ex. 立て前 (たてまえ) - official position; stance
ex. 立食 (りっしょく) - buffet (stand-up meal)

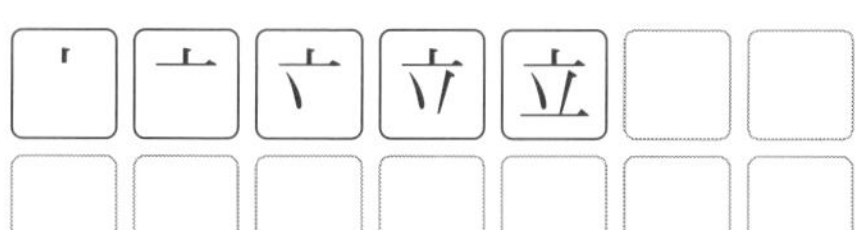

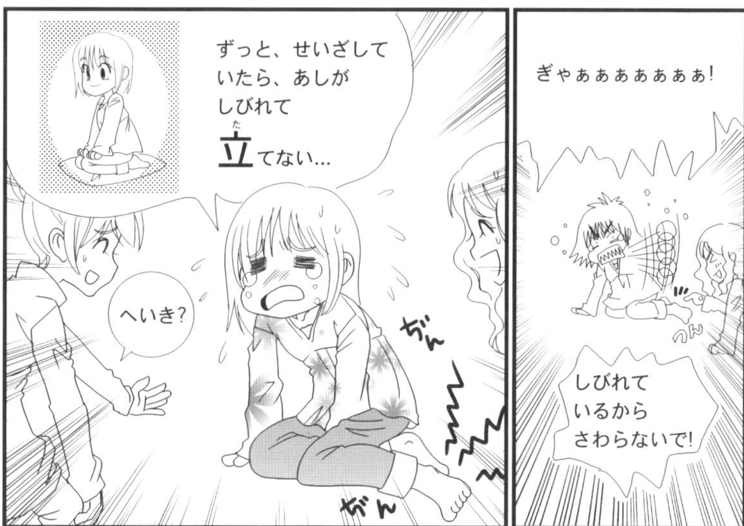

Girl in center: ずっと、せいざして
いたら、あしがしびれて立てない…
My legs fell asleep because I was sitting Japanese-style, and now I can't stand up!

Girl on left: へいき？
Are you OK?

ぢんぢん (sound of numbness)

Girl in center:
ぎゃぁぁぁぁぁぁぁ！
Aaarrrggghhh!

つん (poke)

しびれているから
さわらないで！
Don't touch, they're asleep!

PLEASURE / MUSIC

たの(しい)、たの(しむ)、ガク、ラク

ex. 楽しみ (たのしみ) - enjoyment
ex. 音楽 (おんがく) - music
ex. 楽ちん (らくちん) - easy-going

ヨロヨロヨロ
(sound of difficult pedaling uphill)

Cyclist: 楽ちん！楽ちん！
Easy! Easy!

シャアアアアアア...
(sound of bike zooming downhill)

楽しい！
Fun!

GROUND

チ、ジ

ex. 地下 (ちか) - underground
ex. 地震* (じしん) - earthquake
ex. 地元 (じもと) - local

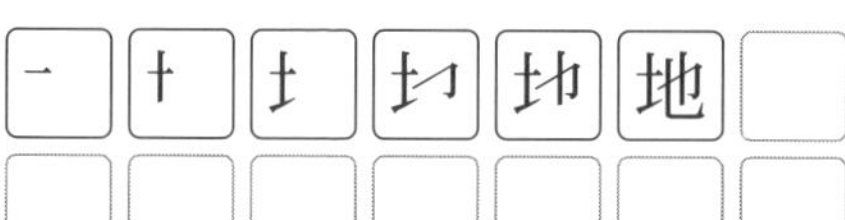

Brother: うわぁぁぁ！
Ahhh!

ぐらぐらぐら (rumble)

地しんだ！
Earthquake!

Brother (dreaming): 地しんだ！すごいゆれだ！
Earthquake! The Big One!

Sister: あそんでー！おきて!
Let's play! Wake up!

ゆっさゆっさ (sound of girl shaking brother)

Brother (awake): うーん… Sh-sure...

NEAR / CLOSE BY

ちか(い)、キン

ex. 近道 (ちかみち) - shortcut
ex. 近年 (きんねん) - recent years
ex. 近所* (きんじょ) - neighborhood

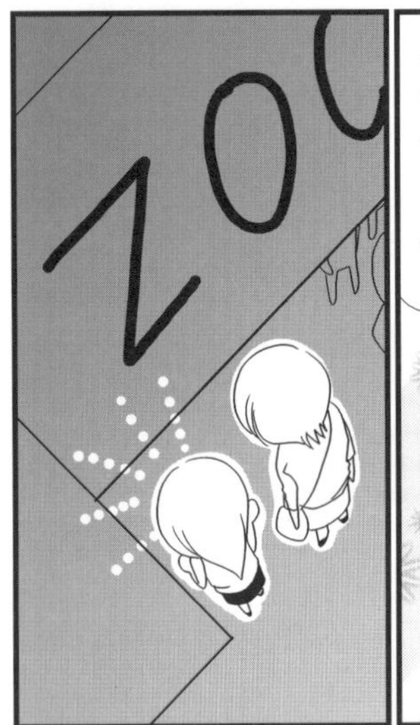

Girl on left: パンダのあかちゃんてぬいぐるみみたいでかわいい！
こんな近くでみたのはじめて。
Baby pandas are so cute, they look just like stuffed toys! I've never seen one up close before.

Girl on right: 近くてラッキー！
We sure are lucky to get so close!

STRENGTH / POWER

ちから、リョク、リキ

ex. 気力 (きりょく) - energy; vitality
ex. 電力 (でんりょく) - electric power
ex. 力持ち* (ちからもち) - muscleman

Boy: ふぬぬぬ…
ぐ…
(grunting noises)

ビンのフタが
あかない！
I can't get this lid off!

Mother: 力まかせに
あけてもだめよ。
Sometimes strength isn't the solution.

Mother: コツさえつかめば、
力なんてひつようない
かもよ。
If you know how to do it, you don't need to use much force at all.

ぱかっ (pop)

TEA

チャ、サ

ex. 茶店 (さてん) - teahouse
ex. 茶色 (ちゃいろ) - brown
ex. 茶道* (さどう) - tea ceremony

シャカシャカシャカ
(shaking noise)

カコーン
(pouring noise)

Woman in kimono: お茶かいってたのしいわね？
Tea ceremony get-togethers sure are fun, aren't they?

Second woman: ほんとう。おまっ茶もおいしいわ。
They sure are. And macha* tea is delicious.

*Macha is a frothy green tea used in traditional tea-pouring ceremonies.

MAKE / CREATE

つく(る)、サク、サ

ex. 工作室 (こうさくしつ) - workshop
ex. 手作り (てづくり) - handmade
ex. 作家* (さっか) - author; novelist

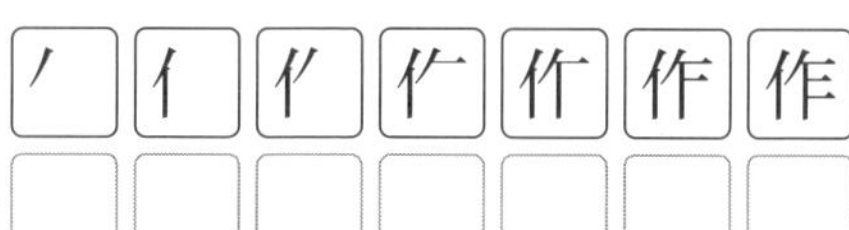

Teacher: みなさん、しゅくだいの作ぶんはかいてきましたか？
Has everyone finished writing the essays I assigned for homework?

Students (in unison): はーい！！
Ye-esss!

Teacher: けんじくんよんでみて。
Kenji, you read yours first.

Kenji: はい。
「はじめて作ったプラモデル」
OK.
"The first plastic model I ever made."

(The symbols 「 」 are used as quotation marks in Japanese.)

STRONG

つよ(い)、つよ(まる)、キョウ、ゴウ

ex. 強大 (きょうだい) - mighty; powerful
ex. 強力 (ごうりき) - enormous strength
ex. 強引* (ごういん) - overbearing

Girl on left: かれって強いよね。また、たいかいでゆうしょうしたんだって。
He sure is strong. He won the tourmanent again.

Girl on right: すごいね!
Incredible!

Girl on left: そのかれをおこるおかあさんはもっと強いよね!
But I'll bet the mother who scolds him is even stronger!

Girl on right: きっとそうだよ。
My thoughts exactly.

HAND

て、シュ

ex. 手袋* (てぶくろ) - glove
ex. 手書き (てがき) - hand-drawn
ex. 握手* (あくしゅ) - handshake

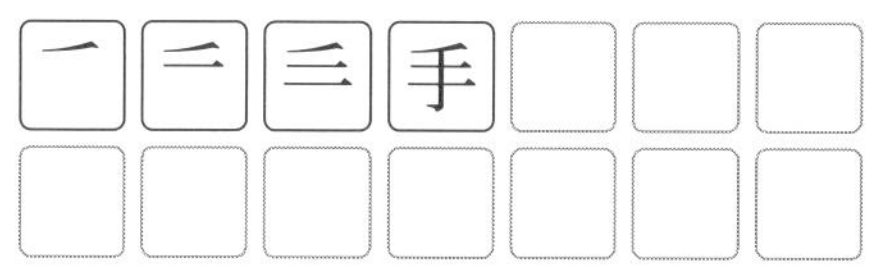

Girl (looking at handicrafts): ぇぇぇ？！
これぜんぶ手づくり？！
What?! All these things are handmade?!

手づくりって、
プロなみよ！
Handmade, just like a pro!

がしっ (sound of holding a hand)

Girl: こんなにごつい…おおきな手なのに。
By this rough and large hand...
すごいよ！すごすぎだよ！
Cool! Really cool!

Craftsman: ありがとう。 Thanks.

てれてれてれ (sound of embarrassment)

STOP

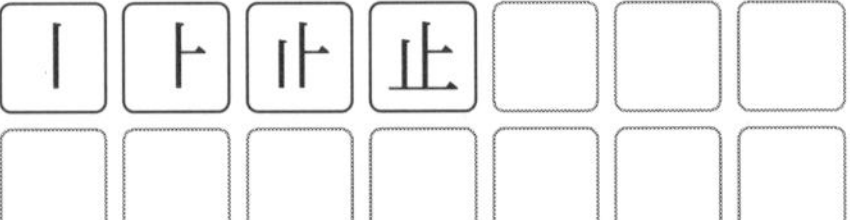

と(まる)、と(める)、シ

ex. 止まれ (とまれ) - stop (traffic) sign
ex. 禁止* (きんし) - prohibition; ban
ex. 中止 (ちゅうし) - suspension

Boy: わっ
Boo!
Girl: ぎゃっ!
Eeek!

Girl: びっくりしたー…しんぞう止まるかと おもったよぉ!
You nearly scared me to death...
I thought my heart had stopped!

Boy: ごめんね。
Sorry.

BIRD

とり、チョウ

ex. 野鳥 (やちょう) - wild bird
ex. 鳥肌* (とりはだ) - goosebumps
ex. 焼き鳥* (やきとり) - grilled chicken

Girl: 鳥ってすべて
とべるのかしら？
Can all birds fly?

Boy: とべない鳥もいるよ。
There are some birds that can't.

Boy: ダチョウとかペンギンは
とべない鳥だね。
Birds such as the ostrich and the penguin can't fly.

Girl: なるほど。
Gotcha.

SUMMER

なつ、カ、ゲ

ex. 夏休み (なつやすみ) - summer vacation
ex. 夏時間 (なつじかん) - summertime
ex. 夏至* (げし) - summer solstice

Schoolboy: きょうからまちにまった夏やすみ！たくさんあそぶぞ。スイカわりしたいな…はなびもしたいな。
Summer vacation finally begins today. I'm gonna have lots of fun! Games... Fireworks.

…でもしゅくだいもたくさんあるよぉ。
...But I still have a ton of homework.

しくしくしくしく…
(sobbing)

どーん (sound of realization)

MEAT / FLESH

ニク

ex. 肉親* (にくしん) - blood relative
ex. 肉球* (にくきゅう) - animal paw
ex. 筋肉* (きんにく) - muscle

Girl: 肉きゅうきもちいい！
ぷにぷにしてる～！
Your paws feel so good!
So squishy!

Girl: きみの肉きゅうはぷにぷにしていて
きもちいいね。やみつきになりそう。
Your paws are soooo squishy and comfortable.
I can't stop feeling them.

Cat: いいめいわくなんだって。
You're really starting to get on my nerves.

FIELD

の、ヤ

ex. 野天 (のてん) - in the open; the open air
ex. 野性* (やせい) - wild (nature)
ex. 野宿* (のじゅく) - camping

Boy: テントのじゅんびはできたね。
You put the tent up.

Girl: きょうはここで野じゅくだね。
We'll camp out here today.

Girl: あ、そうそう。野せいどうぶつにはじゅうぶんきをつけてね。
Oh, by the way, watch out for wild animals.

ドドドドドドド
(sound of fast running)

Girl: あ… Whoa!

RUN

はし(る)、ソウ

ex. 走者* (そうしゃ) - runner
ex. 競走* (きょうそう) - race
ex. 走塁* (そうるい) - base running (baseball)

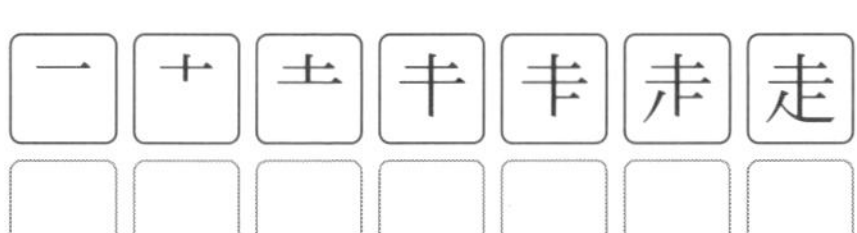

ドタバタドタドタ (sound of running)

Teacher: (surprised)

Teacher: ろうかは走らない！あぶないだろう！きをつけなさい！
No running in the hallway! It's dangerous! Be careful!

Sign: ろうかは走らない (No Running In The Hallway)

ぴたっぴたっ (sound of slower running)

FLOWER

はな、カ

ex. 生け花 (いけばな) - flower arrangement
ex. 花見 (はなみ) - blossom-viewing
ex. 花火 (はなび) - fireworks

Little girl: いちめんお花ばたけだわ！
It's a carpet of flowers!

EARLY / QUICK

はや(い)、はや(まる)、はや(める)、ソウ

ex. 早出 (はやで) - early arrival

ex. 早朝 (そうちょう) - early morning

ex. 早口 (はやくち) - fast talking

Businessman:

早おきするぞ！
I'm gonna get up early tomorrow.

もうこんなじかん。
It's already *what* time?

いそがなきゃ。
I've gotta hurry.

早くもちこくしそう！
たいへんだ。
バスがいっちゃうよ。
I'm already late!
This is terrible.
I'm gonna miss my bus.

SPRING

はる、シュン

ex. 春風 (しゅんぷう) - spring breeze
ex. 春巻き* (はるまき) - spring roll
ex. 青春 (せいしゅん) - youth

一	二	三	声	夫	夫	春
春	春					

Schoolgirl: きせつさきどりで春コートかっちゃった！
I got a head start and bought a new spring coat!

春までまてないもの。
I just couldn't wait till spring.

で…でも、さきどりしすぎたみたい…さむいよ。
B...but, I think I jumped the gun. It's cold out.

ガチガチガチ (shivering)

春はまだ？ Is it spring yet?

DAYTIME / NOON

ひる、チュウ

ex. 昼間 (ひるま) - daytime

ex. 昼休み (ひるやすみ) - lunchtime

ex. 昼寝* (ひるね) - nap

Schoolboy: きょうの昼ごはんはなんにしようかな…
I wonder what I should have for lunch today...

まようなぁ。うーん。ラーメン、いや、セットも…
I can't decide. Hmmm. Ramen, nah, or maybe a lunch set...

トントン (finger-tapping)

Schoolgirl: はやくしないと昼やすみおわっちゃうよ。
You better hurry or lunchtime will be over.

WIDE

ひろ(い)、ひろ(げる)、コウ

ex. 広大 (こうだい) - huge

ex. 広間 (ひろま) - large room; hall

ex. 広場* (ひろば) - plaza

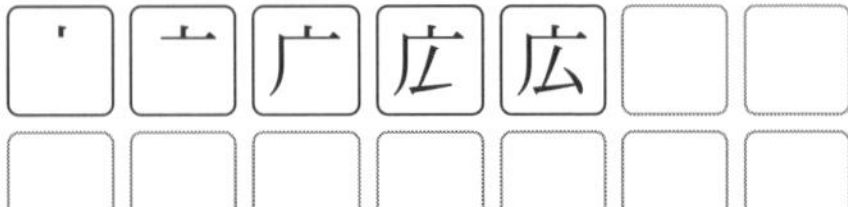

Boy: うわー… 広いへやだね。
Wow... It sure is a wide room.

WINTER

ふゆ、トウ

ex. 冬休み (ふゆやすみ) - winter vacation
ex. 冬眠* (とうみん) - hibernation
ex. 冬至* (とうじ) - winter solstice

Little boy: 冬っていろいろ
イベントもあって
たのしいけど…
There are lots of fun events to go to during the winter...

Little boy: さむいからくまみたいに
冬みんしたいなぁ。
But it's so cold I just want to hibernate like a bear.

Big sister: いいから、おきなさい。
Come on, outta bed.

OLD

ふる(い)、ふる(す)、コ

ex. 古風 (こふう) - old customs
ex. 古物* (こぶつ) - antique
ex. 古寺* (ふるでら) - old temple

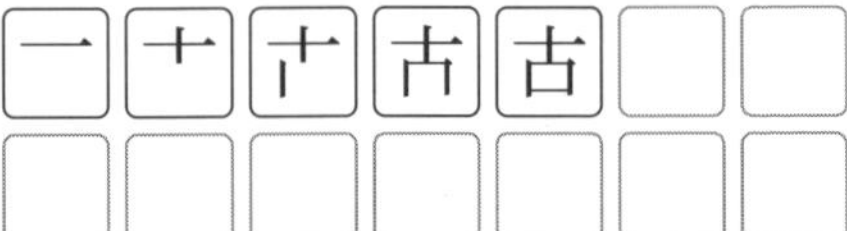

Boy: 古いおかねだなぁ。
Hey, it's an old coin.

Teacher: いまから300ねん
くらいまえの
おかねよ。
It's actually about
300 years old.

Boy: そんなに古いの？！
It's that old?!

LETTER / WRITINGS

ブン、モン

ex. 文章* (ぶんしょう) - sentence
ex. 文字 (もじ) - letter (of alphabet); character
ex. 文化* (ぶんか) - culture; civilization

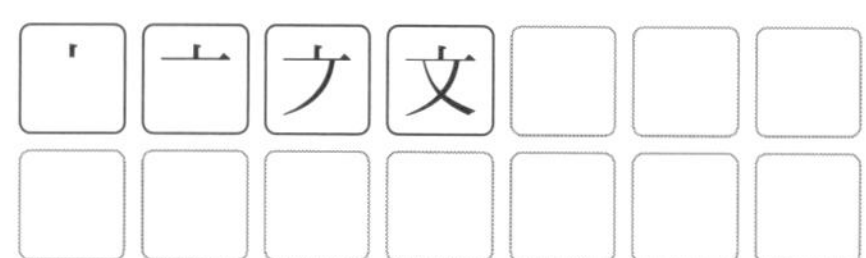

Boy: うーん…
文しょうもんだいってにがてだなぁ。
Ugh...
I don't like long-sentence homework problems.

文しょうもんだいで
なくてもにがてだけど…
Then again, I don't like the short-sentence ones either...

トホホ…
Sigh...

ENDEAVOUR

ベン

ex. 勉強 (べんきょう) - study
ex. 勉学 (べんがく) - pursuit of knowledge
ex. 勉強家 (べんきょうか) - diligent student

Schoolgirl: けんじくんて勉きょう
ねっしんね。
Kenji, you really enjoy studying, don't you?

Kenji: がくせいたるもの
勉きょうがほんぎょう
だとおもっていますから。
As a student, I believe it's our duty to study.

Schoolgirl: おぉ。 Yeah.
ぱちぱちぱち (clapping)

TOWN

まち、チョウ

ex. 町会 (ちょうかい) - town council
ex. 町民* (ちょうみん) - townspeople
ex. 町外れ (まちはずれ) - outskirts of town

Girl: はなやみどりがたくさんあって すてき。とてもいい町ね。
All these flowers and plants make it so beautiful. This is such a nice city.

Boy: 町ぜんたいでとりくんでいるんだ。
The entire city works together to keep it looking this way.

Girl: そうなんだ...
You don't say...

SHOP / STORE

みせ、テン

ex. 本店 (ほんてん) - main store; head office

ex. 店員* (てんいん) - store clerk

ex. 店先 (みせさき) - storefront

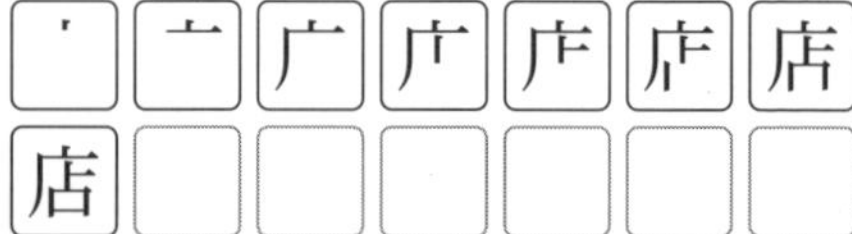

First girl: すてき！
これぜんぶ、あなたが
つくったの？
How beautiful!
You made all of these?

Second girl: そうよ。
That's right.

Second girl: しょうらいは、
じぶんでお店をひらきたいんだ。
Someday I want to open my own store.

First girl: がんばってね！
Good luck!

STREET / ROAD

みち、ドウ

ex. 道路* (どうろ) - road; highway
ex. 道辺* (みちべ) - roadside
ex. 柔道* (じゅうどう) - judo

Girl: ねぇ、この道ほんとうにあっているの？
Are you sure this is the right road?

Boy: 道はあっている！はずなんだけど…なぁ…
This is the right road! I think so, anyway...

Boy: やっぱり、道にまよったかなぁ…
Um, we might be on the wrong road...

Girl: ぜったいまよっているわよ！
We're definitely lost!

ROOM

むろ、シツ

ex. 室内* (しつない) - in the room
ex. 教室 (きょうしつ) - classroom
ex. 室外 (しつがい) - outdoors

'	'ᐟ	宀	宀	宀	宏	宝
室	室					

Teacher: これからきょう室のおそうじをはじめます。みんなでつくえといすをかたづけてー。
All right, it's time to clean our classroom. Everyone move your desks and chairs.

はい、がんばって！
That's right, attaboy!

(In Japan, students—not janitors—are responsible for the upkeep of their classrooms. At the end of the schoolday, the children mop the floors and clean the windows. These activities teach the importance of teamwork and help instill school pride.)

EYE

め、モク

ex. 目ぐすり (めぐすり) - eyedrops

ex. 目途* (めど) - outlook

ex. 科目* (かもく) - school subject

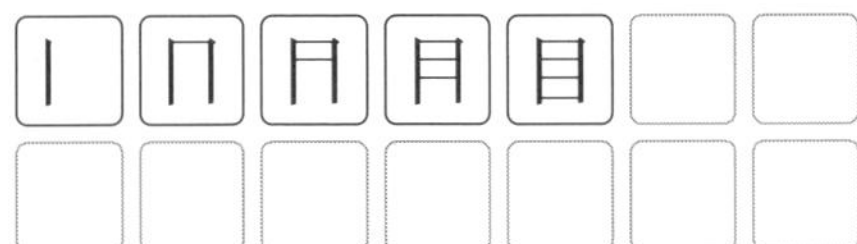

Schoolgirl: おはよう…
Morning...

Classmate: わっ！
どうしたの？！目のまわりが
すごくはれてるよ。
Whoa! What happened? Your eyes are all puffy.

Schoolgirl: きのう、すごくなける
えいがをたくさんみちゃって…
I watched a real tear-jerker of a movie yesterday...

Classmate: なかないで！もっと目の
まわりがはれちゃうよ。
Don't cry now! Your eyes will get worse.

ORIGIN

もと、ゲン、ガン

ex. 元祖* (がんそ) - originator; pioneer
ex. 元日 (がんじつ) - New Year's Day
ex. 元気 (げんき) - healthy

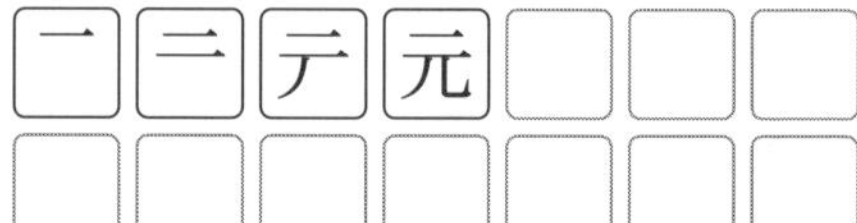

ごちゃごちゃ
(roughhousing noises)

Mother: まぁっ！
こんなにちらかして！
My goodness! What a mess!

Mother: 元どおりにかたづけなさい！
きちんとよ？！わかったなら
へんじをして！
Put everything back the way it was!
You hear?! Answer me if you understand!

Boys: は…はーい。
Y...Yes.

COMPANY

やしろ、シャ

ex. 社長 (しゃちょう) - company president
ex. 社会科* (しゃかいか) - social studies
ex. 社 (やしろ) - Shinto shrine

Teacher: きょうの社かいのじゅぎょうは…
For today's social studies lesson...

Teacher: かい社けんがくです！
...we will visit a company!

Sign: かい社 (Company)

Teacher: 社ちょうさんです！
There's the company president!

Students (in unison): こんにちはー
Hello-ooo!

EVENING

ゆう

ex. 夕方 (ゆうがた) - evening
ex. 夕日 (ゆうひ) - evening (setting) sun
ex. 夕刊* (ゆうかん) - evening newspaper

Mother: きょうはきれいな夕ひね。
It sure is a beautiful evening.

Boy: おかあさん、みて。
かげがこんなにながいよ。
Look, mom. Our shadows are really long.

NIGHT

よ、よる、ヤ

ex. 夜空 (よぞら) - night sky
ex. 夜中 (よなか) - midnight
ex. 夜食 (やしょく) - midnight snack

Girl: なんでオバケって夜くらいしかでてこないのかしら…
I wonder why ghosts only come out at night...

Boy: なんだ、そんなことかんたんだよ！
That's an easy one!

Boy: ひるまででてきてもこわくないもん。だから夜なんだよ。
They wouldn't be scary when it's bright out, so they come out at night.

ドキッ (sound of shock)

じー… (sound of staring)

Girl: それもそうね。 That makes sense.

TAKE THE TEST!

The Japanese Language Proficiency Test has been held annually throughout the world since 1984. Administered by the Japanese government and the nonprofit Japan Foundation, the test evaluates and certifies the proficiency of non-native speakers of Japanese. There are four levels to the examination: Level 4 for beginners, Level 3 for intermediate students, Level 2 for those who are functionally literate in Japanese, and Level 1 for experts.

This book features 80 of the kanji students need to know to pass Level 3 of the JLPT. Subsequent volumes in Manga University's *Kanji de Manga* series will help students prepare for the higher levels.

For more information about the Japanese Language Proficiency Test, including examination locations in your country, please visit the Japan Foundation's "JLPT Communications Square" website at http://momo.jpf.go.jp/jlpt/e/about_e.html.

PRACTICE SECTION

KANJI INDEX

The 80 kanji featured in this volume of *Kanji de Manga* are indexed here based on their *on-yomi* and *kun-yomi* readings. This makes it easy to look up any kanji for which you know a pronunciation but cannot remember how the character is written. Because most kanji have more than one reading, you will find those characters listed multiple times in this index.

GLENN KARDY is the editor of several volumes in the renowned *How to Draw Manga* series of art-instruction guides, including *Getting Started*, the first book of its kind to be used at major universities in both the United States (UCLA) and Japan (Waseda). Glenn lives in the Tokyo suburb of Kawaguchi City with his wife, their daughter and a collection of Oakland A's bobblehead dolls.

CHIHIRO HATTORI, niece of legendary manga artist Eiichi Fukui, was a graphics designer at Tokyo-based TechnoArt before turning her attention full-time to her manga career. Chihiro and her husband live in Yokohama, where they enjoy fine food, fast cars and high fashion.

Front cover illustration by Honepanda
Back cover illustration by Chihiro Hattori
Project coordinator: Kanako Umehara
Translator: Kahori Hirano
Copy editor: Mari Oyama
Layout assistant: Hideyasu Mitsui

Special thanks to Edward Mazza

MANGA UNIVERSITY presents...

A fun, easy way to learn the ABCs of Japanese!

TOKYO SAN FRANCISCO

Manga University presents ... Kana de Manga
A Fun, Easy Way to Learn the ABCs of Japanese

ISBN 4-921205-01-9

Published by Japanime Co. Ltd.
3-31-18 Nishi-Kawaguchi
Kawaguchi-shi, Saitama 332-0021
Japan

First edition June 2004
Second edition December 2004
Third edition October 2005

Printed in Japan

Emily へ
Daddy から

CONTENTS

FOREWORD

Learning the Japanese phonetic alphabets of hiragana and katakana is perhaps the single most useful thing any visitor to Japan can do. The reason is that restaurant names, foreign terms and transportation signs use these visual alphabets. If you can pronounce the sound of these characters, you can get around easily and have more fun in Japan.

Hiragana (cursive form) and katakana (squared form) are the true "ABCs of Japanese," as they can be used to write words as well as complete sentences. Children in Japan learn to read and write hiragana and katakana (collectively known as kana) long before they are introduced to Chinese characters, or kanji. Also, most manga comic books targeted toward the youngest readers in Japan are written completely in kana.

Each kana page in this book has an easy-to-grasp manga cartoon image representing a sound that begins with the hiragana or katakana character featured prominently at the top of the page. A brief informative explanation accompanies each drawing; the English equivalent of the word is given; and there is a work area where the person studying can practice writing the kana forms.

This Manga University book has been prepared to make learning the phonetic sounds of Japanese kana systems both fun and effective. Educators know that language learning is enhanced through images and

associations. This book builds on these principles by linking Japanese kana characters to Japanese images that anyone can readily identify.

So, don't waste any time! Make the investment. Once you master the kana characters in this book you will find a whole new world of Japan will be opened up to you.

Ronald A. Morse
Professor of Japan Studies, University of Nevada, Las Vegas

INTRODUCTION

Congratulations! When you purchased this book, you took a step into a whole new world – the world of reading and writing in Japanese. It's a world of endless possibility, and you'll find new doors opening as you learn each new character. Soon, you'll be able to read your favorite manga comics in their original language. You'll burst through the language barrier as you make Japanese friends online. And when you visit Japan, you'll be able to read signs, menus, maps and more on your own. There are hundreds of reasons to learn Japanese, and mastery of its most basic writing system is the best way to get started.

The two systems we'll be focusing on, hiragana and katakana, are phonetic syllabaries. Each one has 46 characters, called kana, which function much like English letters in that each has a specific pronunciation. Complete sentences can be written in kana by people who don't know kanji, the far more complex set of characters based on Chinese ideographs. Kana can be used to unlock these kanji characters, and are learned first by Japanese children and students of the language before they move on to kanji. By some estimates, there are more than 50,000 different kanji, but only about 2,000 are officially recognized by the Japanese Ministry of Education as frequently used characters. A fourth script, called romaji, is used to make Japanese readable to others by converting the characters into English, or "roman," letters. For instance, the title of this book, "Kana de Manga," is the romaji, or romanized, form of what would be written as かなでマンガ in Japanese.

USAGE AND PRONUNCIATION

In general, hiragana is used to write native Japanese words and inflections, while katakana is used to make foreign words readable to the Japanese.

Katakana is also often used for the names of plants and animals. In both hiragana and katakana, each character represents a syllable, as opposed to letters in the English language. There are more kana than letters, of course, but don't worry – they're quite easy to memorize. To help you get started, we've written each kana in romaji on the charts in the front and back of this book.

There are five basic vowel sounds in spoken Japanese:

a as in ***ah***
i as in s**ee**
u as in y***ou***
e as in n**e**xt
o as in ***oh***

Sometimes the vowel sounds are long. In hiragana, these long sounds are indicated by the addition of あ, い, う, え or お following the vowel. For instance, both the first and second vowel sounds in "Tokyo" are long, as the Japanese capital is actually closer to a four-syllable word in Japanese than the three-syllable word it has become in English. Thus, in hiragana, Tokyo is written とうきょう, with each う indicating an extended "o" sound.

In katakana, these elongated vowels are indicated by a long dash. The word "cheerleader," for example, is written チアリーダー, with the dashes elongating the "ri" and "da" sounds to match the Japanese pronunciation of "leader."

There are different ways to indicate the elongated vowels in romaji. For hiragana, this book uses a modified version of the Hepburn system: Long vowels indicated by an additional い or あ are romanized as ii and aa, respectively, but those featuring an additional う, え or お are romanized with just a single u, e or o.

It is highly unusual to use Hepburn romanization for katakana. Instead, the actual foreign spelling of the word is usually used. For instance, the word トイレットペーパー is simply "toilet paper" when romanized. But we need to work on our pronunciation as we learn katakana, so we're also going to include an unorthodox form of romanization. As a result, トイレットペーパー becomes not only "toilet paper," but also "toirettopeepaa." This type of romanization will look downright weird to those familiar with romaji, so don't get used to it. In fact, once you've learned kana, you should avoid romaji altogether – you won't need it anymore anyway!

Consonant sounds are virtually the same as those heard in English, with the

following exceptions. The "f" sound is considerably softer in Japanese than in English. And the "l" sound, of course, is almost nonexistent in Japanese, with a Japanese approximation falling somewhere between a "d" and an "r" to English-trained ears, and usually romanized with an "r."

Both hiragana and katakana make use of diacritic symbols called dakuten and handakuten to change the sounds of consonants. These modified characters are included in the charts at the front and back of this book.

A dakuten looks like this ゛ and turns k into g, t into d, s into z and h into b.

A handakuten looks like this ゜ and is used almost exclusively to turn h into p.

And a small つ (for hiragana) or ツ (for katakana) placed before a character doubles the consonant. For example, "kippu" (the Japanese word for ticket), is written as きっぷ in hiragana, while the English word "knock" (nokku in romaji) is written as ノック in katakana.

Finally, remember that all Japanese words end either in a vowel, or a consonant that can sound like either an "m" or an "n," depending on the word. This consonant is represented in hiragana as ん and in katakana as ン. There are no other consonant endings in Japanese.

STROKE ORDER

Now we're almost ready to start writing our kana, but it's important to learn the proper stroke order. This is essential to Japanese penmanship. Characters written using the wrong stroke order tend to look sloppy to trained eyes – and soon, your eyes will be able to tell the difference as well.

"Kana de Manga" makes this easy: At the bottom of each page is a practice area with numbered arrows indicating the sequence and direction of each stroke. In general, strokes are written from top to bottom, and left to right, with horizontal strokes followed by vertical strokes. Let's take a look at the hiragana character ま:

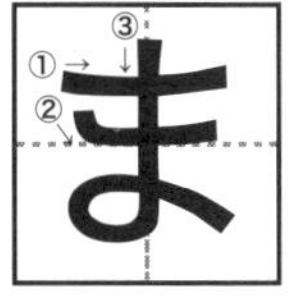

Here, the first stroke goes from left to right, the second goes a bit down before sweeping from left to right, and the final stroke goes straight down before looping up and around from the left. Top to bottom, left to right, horizontal before vertical.

Some kana are written in a single stroke that may change directions several times. These are among the easiest to write. A good example of this is the hiragana character る:

The stroke begins at the upper left and climbs slightly to the right before angling down in a long stroke to the left, then circling down toward the right and back to the left before looping again to the right. Single-stroke kana are among the easiest to write.

Multi-stroke kana may include a stroke that changes directions several times, like the hiragana character ね:

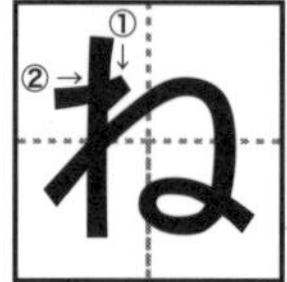

The first stroke is a straight line going from top to bottom. The second stroke juts from the left to the right before entering a sharp angle downward to the left, then sweeping back up to the right and down again, finishing in a loop that circles from left to right.

Katakana characters consist mainly of straight, angled strokes, and thus are very easy to memorize and write. Even the four-stroke character ネ is fairly simple:

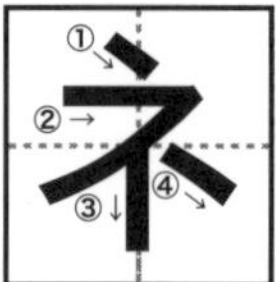

The first stroke is a short, angled line moving from left to right. The next stroke goes horizontally from left to right before reversing into a downward angle to the left. The third stroke travels down from the second, while the fourth moves in the same direction as the first.

There is much more to the use of hiragana and katakana than what we've just explained, of course. You can study Japanese for years, and still find new things to learn. The goal of "Kana de Manga" is simple: to introduce you to hiragana and katakana, help familiarize you with Japanese writing, and have a little fun doing it.

それでは、はじめましょう！(Sore dewa, hajimemasho! So, let's begin!)

HIRAGANA AND KATAKANA

あしあと

a**shiato**

footprints

If you really want to learn how to read and write Japanese, you're going to have to get your feet wet. The first step is to study ひらがな (hiragana) and カタカナ (katakana), which is what this book will help you do. Take your time and don't get frustrated if you stumble now and then. Oh, and watch out for that puddle of mud!

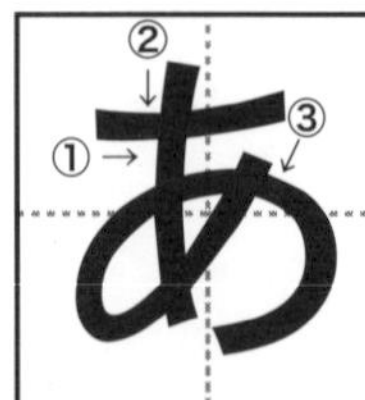

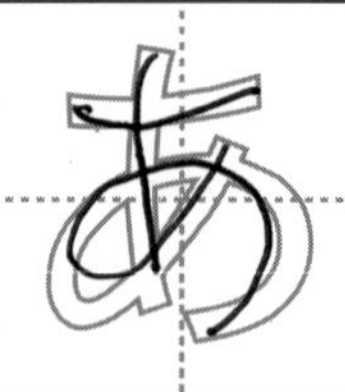

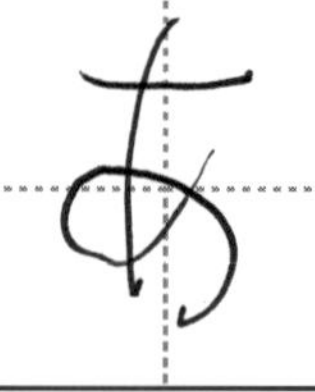

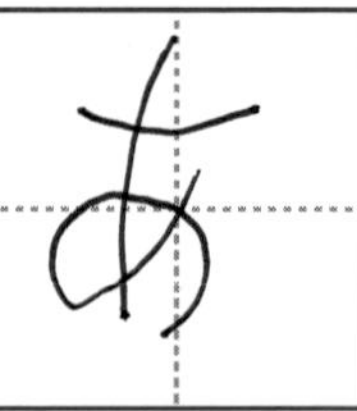

アルファベット

***a**rufuabetto*

alphabet

Remember how easy it was to learn the ABCs when you were a child? Well, memorizing kana is just as simple! Invent word games, make flash cards, and perhaps even write a "kana song." Keep at it, and soon you too will be ぺらぺら (perapera; fluent) in Japanese.

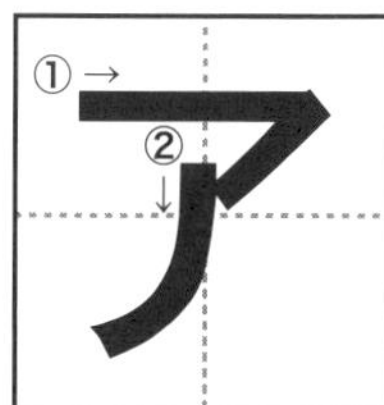

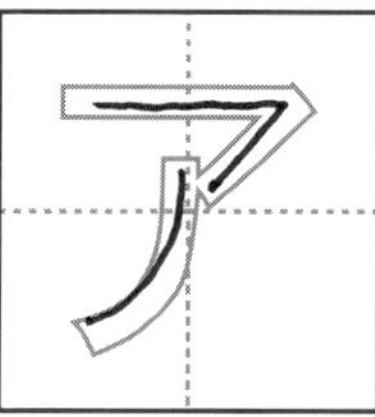

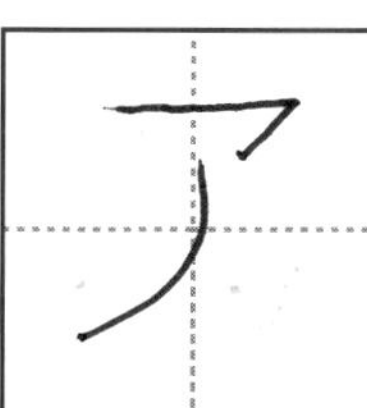

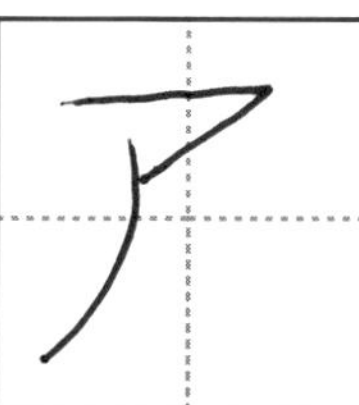

いそぐ

i**sogu**

to hurry

Hey, buddy, what's the rush? Have you already memorized the first two かな (kana) characters in this book? No? Then turn back the page and work on あ and ア before you get too far ahead of yourself! Don't worry, we'll still be here when you catch up.

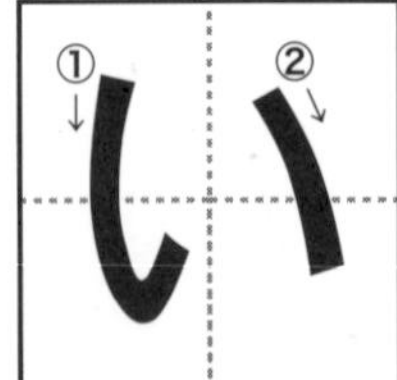

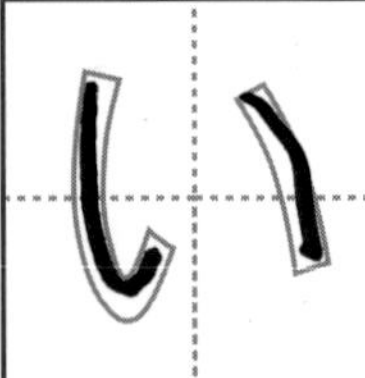

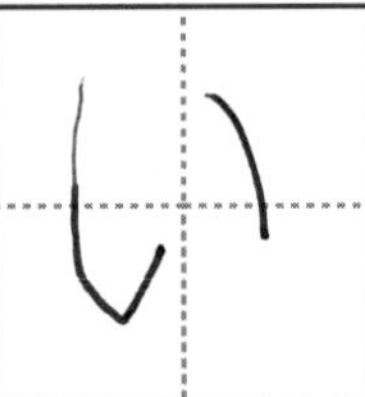

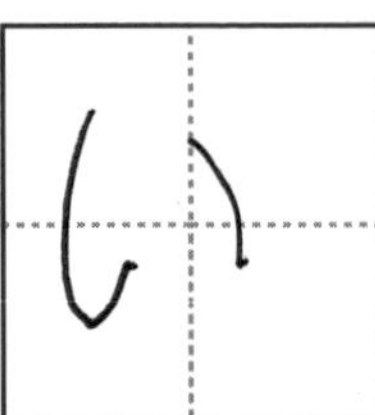

イヤリング

***i**yaringu*

earring

If diamonds really are a girl's best friend, then a lost earring is quite possibly her worst enemy, especially when she's already running late for a date. When she finally finds the elusive item, she is likely to shout あった (atta; there it is). The Japanese word for "lost item" is おとしもの (otoshimono).

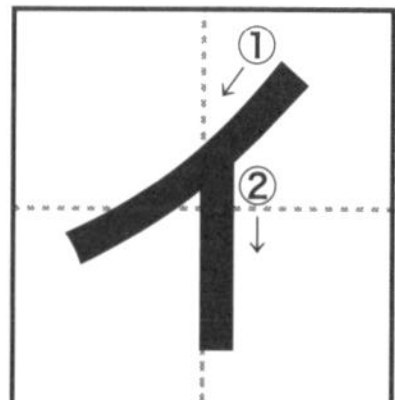

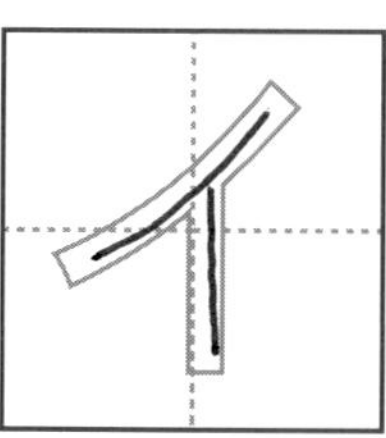

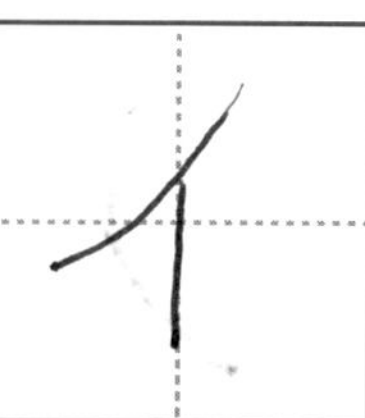

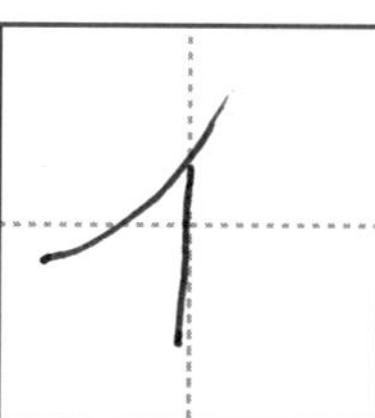

うみ

***u**mi*

beach, sea

Nobody said that learning にほんご (nihongo; Japanese) would be a day at the beach, but it's still lots of fun! And here's an interesting fact: Japan is a しょとう (shoto; chain of islands) with more than 18,000 miles of coastline. That's enough room for one big beach bash!

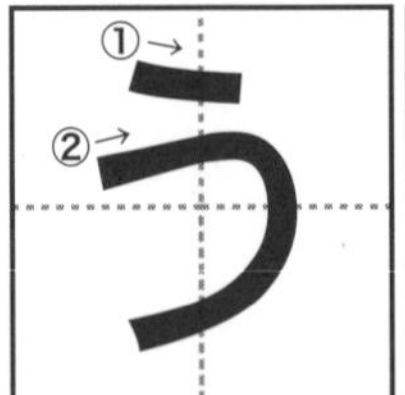

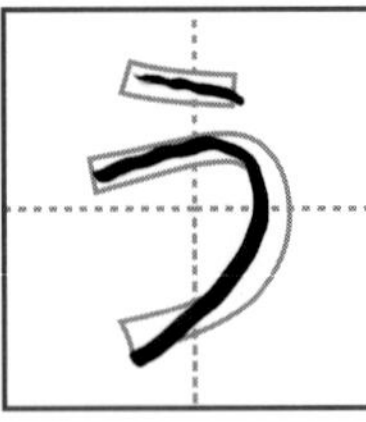

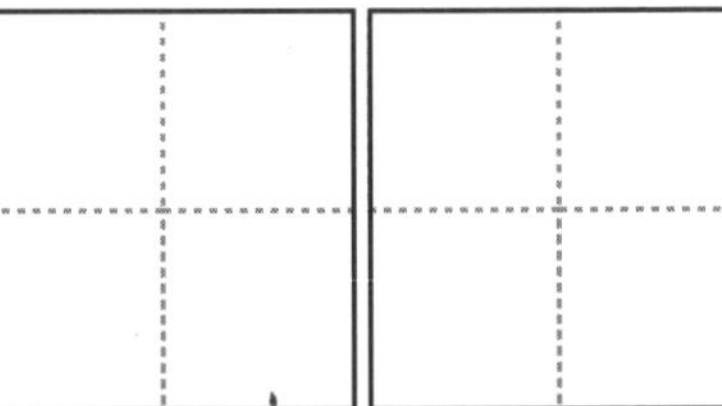

ウインク

***u*inku**

wink

A wink is worth a thousand words—especially when it's made by a びしょうじょ (bishojo; beautiful girl). The guy pictured here, though, seems to be a bit はずかしい (hazukashii; embarrassed) by his flirtatious friend.

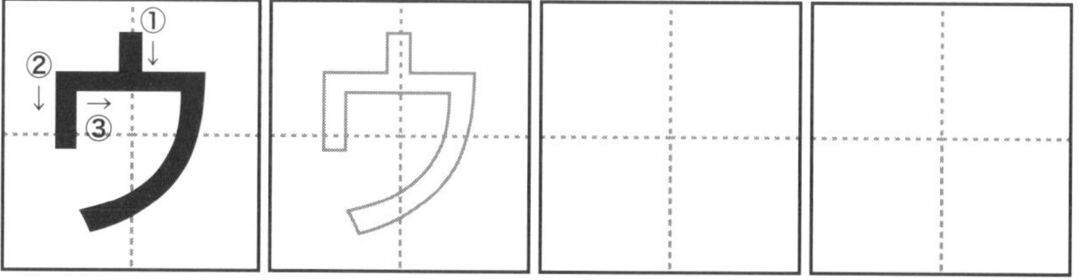

えほん

ehon

picture book

Parents in Japan read to their children many of the same fairy tales enjoyed by toddlers in North America and Europe, including シンデレラものがたり (Shinderera Monogatari), better known as "The Story of Cinderella." Of course, the Japanese have their own folk stories, including the curiously titled ももたろう (Momotaro), or "Peach Boy."

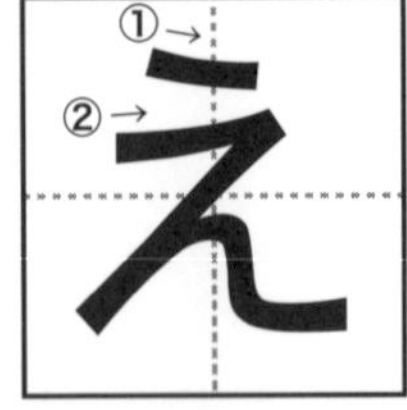

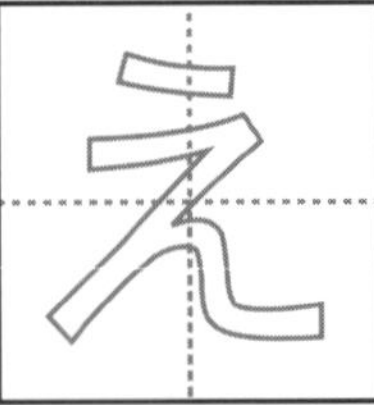

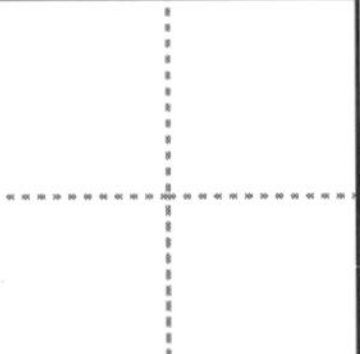

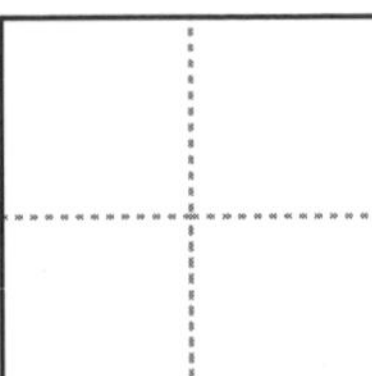

エラー

era

error

The Great American Pastime is also a hit in Japan, where やきゅう (yakyu; baseball) is played year-round. High school tournaments are held twice a year at Koushien Stadium and televised nationwide, with virtually every household in the country tuned in. It's the last place a player wants to misjudge a ground ball.

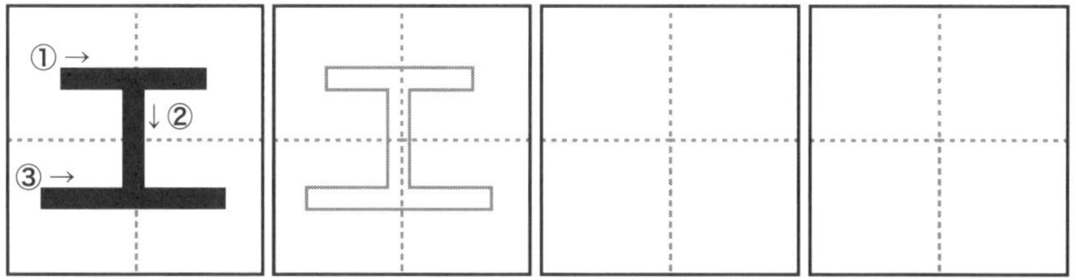

おんせん

onsen

hot spring

Among Japan's most popular tourist attractions are hot-spring resorts where wild さる (saru; monkeys) soak with the tourists. It's usually a very calm and pleasant experience. However, once in a while the monkeys go bananas and attack their guests. So, if you ever visit one of these places, bathe at your own risk!

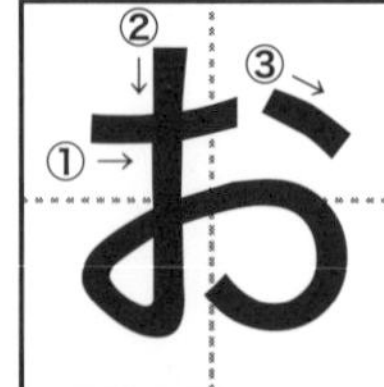

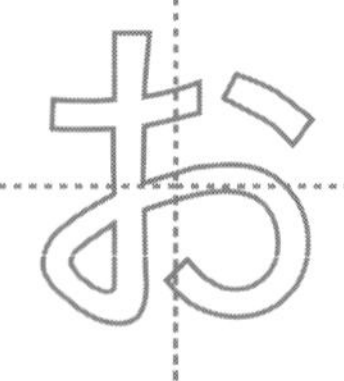

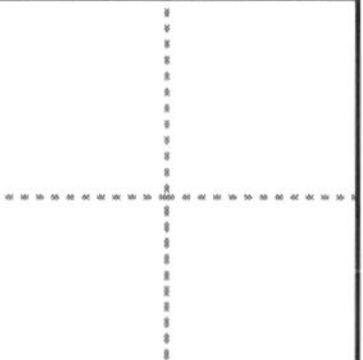

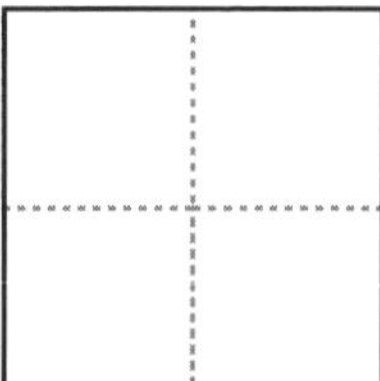

オルゴール

***o*rugoru**

music box

Orgel, the Dutch (and German) word for organ, becomes オルゴール in Japanese, and is used to describe all types of music boxes, from simple jewelry containers to elaborate musical figurines from 19th-century ヨーロッパ (Yoroppa; Europe).

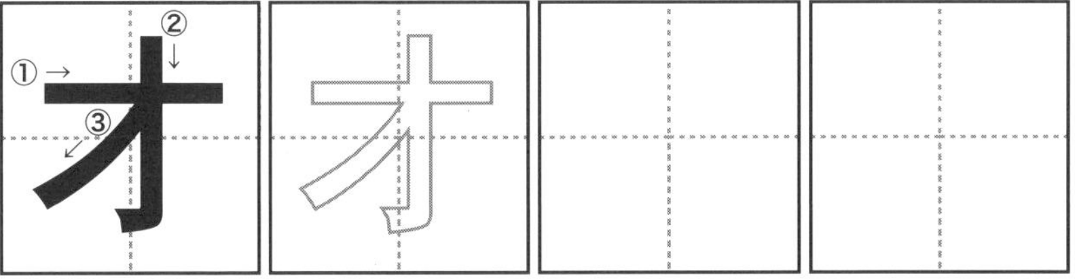

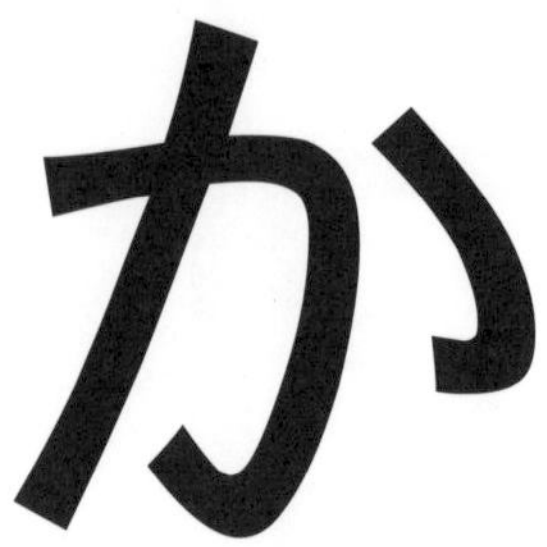

か

ka

mosquito

Planning a summertime trip to Japan? Be sure to have plenty of mosquito-repellant on hand! The pesky insects are everywhere, and they're always hungry! Fortunately, they are more an itch-inducing nuisance than anything else, and there is no risk of マラリア (mararia; malaria) in Japan.

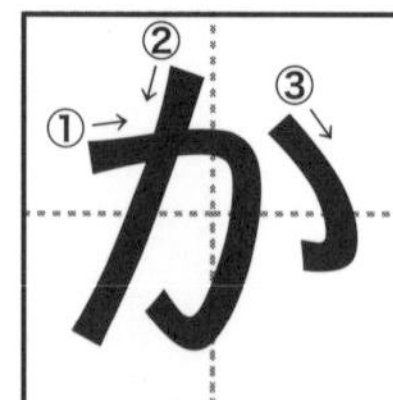

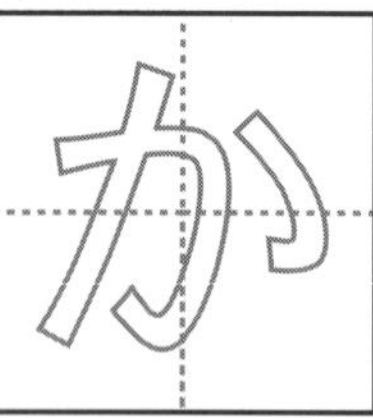

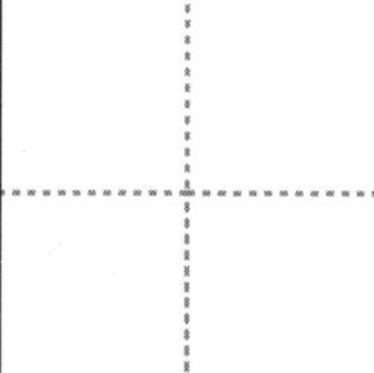

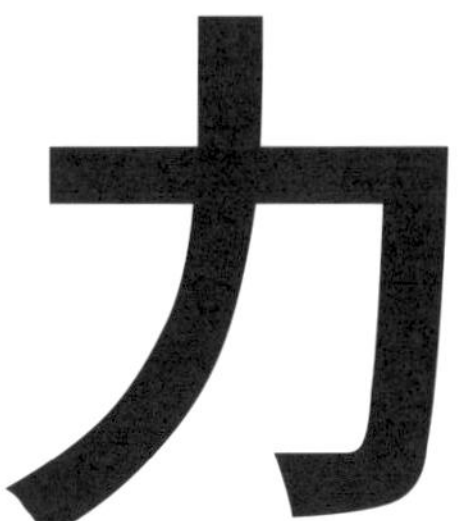

カラオケ

***ka*raoke**

karaoke

In Japan, everyone wants to be a singer. That explains the popularity of karaoke clubs, where would-be rock 'n' rollers gather to give their vocal cords a workout. Few, however, have the stuff it takes to become a star, and their audiences (usually consisting of close friends) often leave the clubs screaming みみがいたい (mimi ga itai; my ears hurt)!

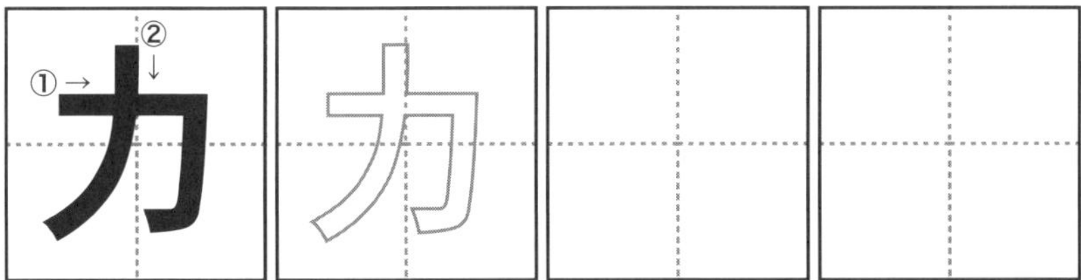

きもの

***ki*mono**

kimono

Meet the Tone Twins, リナちゃん (Rina-chan) and サキちゃん (Saki-chan). In addition to sharing the same birthday, these two fun-loving sisters from Tokyo attend the same school (Manga University, of course), shop at the same stores, and sometimes even date the same guys!
They also share a keen sense of style, especially when it comes to Japanese kimono. Rina favors the refined look of earth-tone silk, while Saki prefers bright floral patterns. Lucky for us—otherwise, it would be impossible to tell them apart!

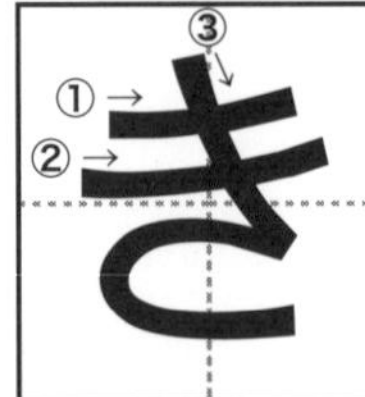

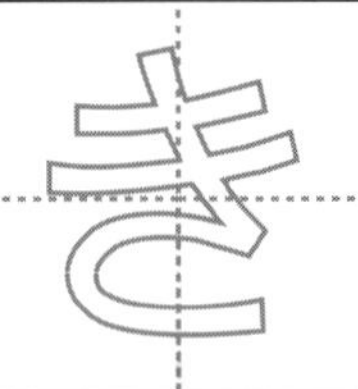

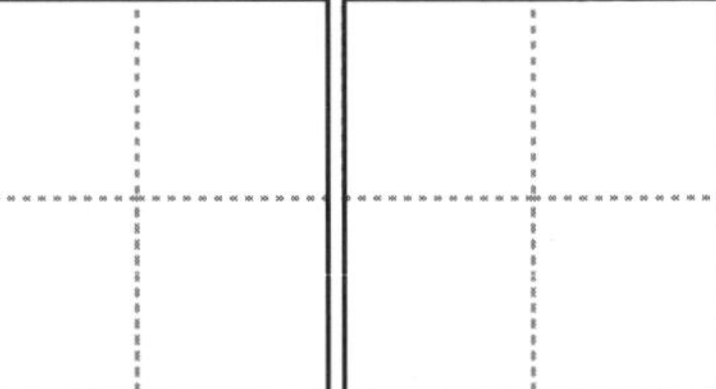

キノコ

***ki*noko**

mushroom

The names of plants and animals are often written in katakana, though hiragana is also used. Mushroom, for instance, can be written as either キノコ or きのこ. We like 'em both ... especially on top of ピザ (piza; pizza).

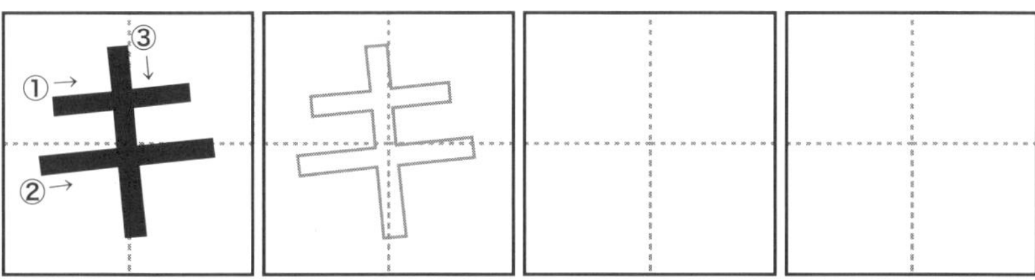

***ku*tsu**

shoes

There's nothing that makes a little guy feel like a big man more than walking around in his daddy's shoes. Let's just hope he remembers to take them off before stepping foot into a Japanese home, though, where wearing shoes is だめ (dame), a no-no.

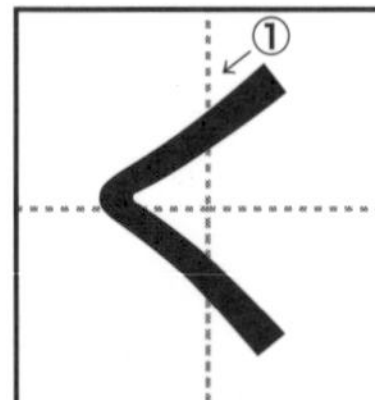

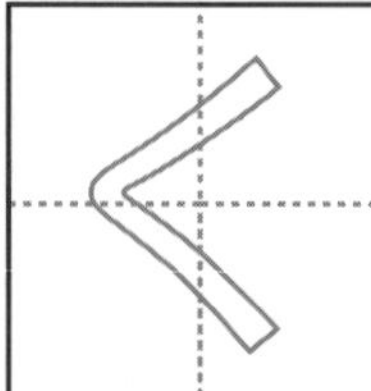

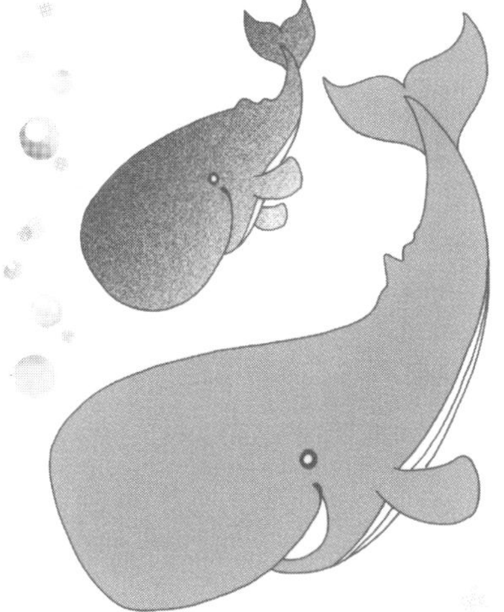

クジラ

***ku**jira*

whale

Japan is one of the few nations of the world to practice the hunting of whales despite a worldwide ban on the activity. However, there is a significant animal-rights movement in the country that is trying to get the government to change its policy and protect the ぜつめつきぐしゅ (zetsumetsukigushu; endangered species).

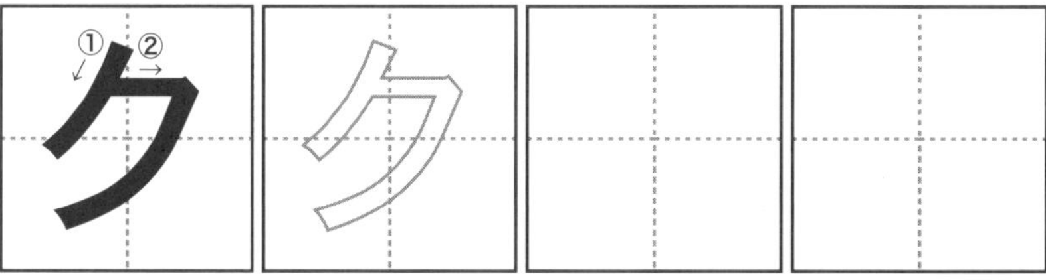

けいたいでんわ

ketaidenwa

cellular phone

Although convenient and easy to use, cellular phones are also the source of much irritation in Japan. For instance, there's nothing more frustrating to a young guy than when he gives his でんわばんごう (denwabango; phone number), to a pretty girl he meets at a party, and she never calls him back!

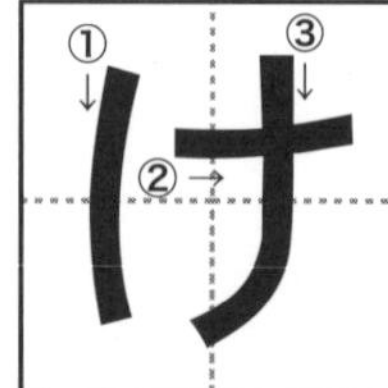

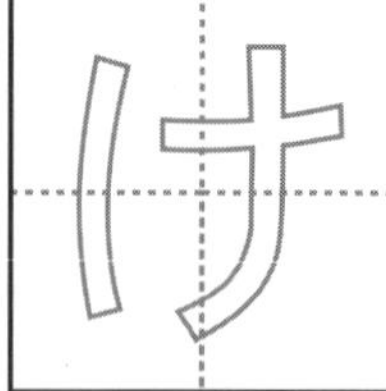

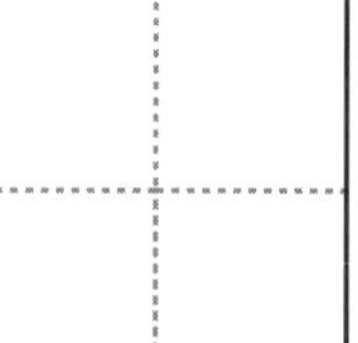

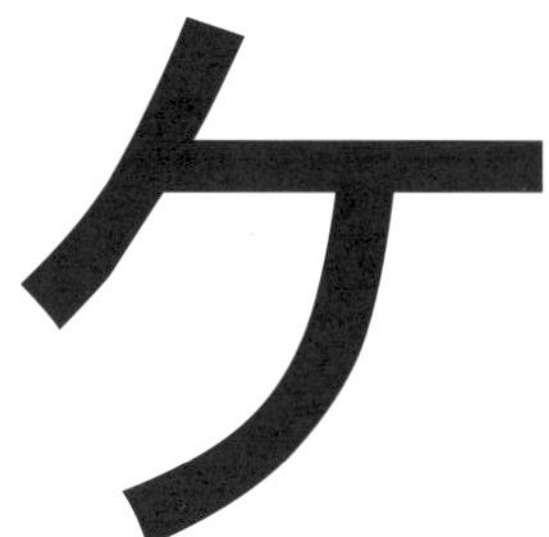

***ke**ki*

cake

Now we know why the pretty girl never called our ともだち (tomodachi; friend) on the previous page. She's already involved in a long-term relationship ... with the bakery-next-door!

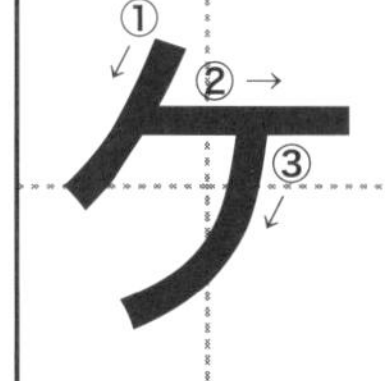
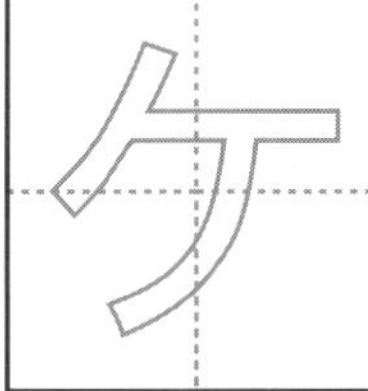

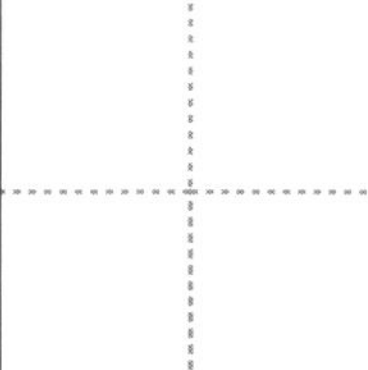

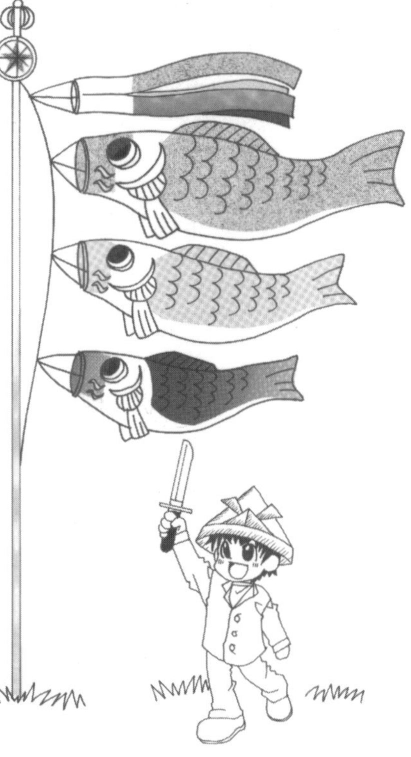

こいのぼり

***ko*inobori**

carp-shaped streamer

To the Japanese, the こい (koi; carp), is a symbol of courage and strength, traits they hope to instill in their sons. So, during the weeks leading up to the こどものひ (Kodomo no Hi; Children's Day) holiday in May, parents proudly display carp-shaped のぼり (nobori; streamers) outside their homes to honor their sons. The colorful windsocks are a remarkable sight to behold, and one of the enduring memories of a springtime trip to Japan.

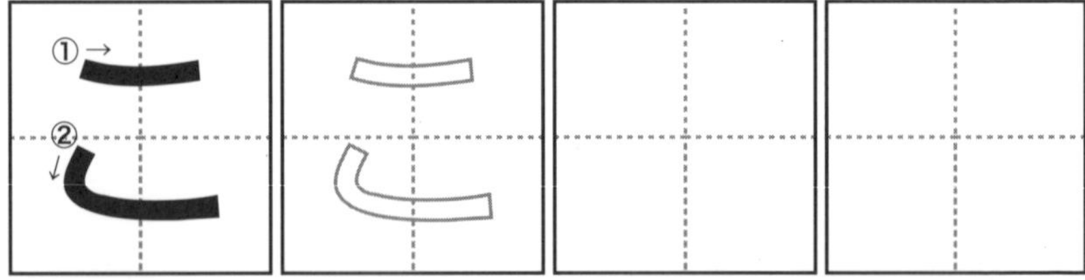

コアラ

***ko**ara*

koala bear

There aren't any koala bears in Japan (except for those in zoos), but there are plenty of koala cookies. コアラのマーチ (Koara no Maachi; March of the Koalas), is a popular brand of chocolate-filled biscuits shaped like tiny koala bears. Absolutely おいしい (oishii; delicious)!

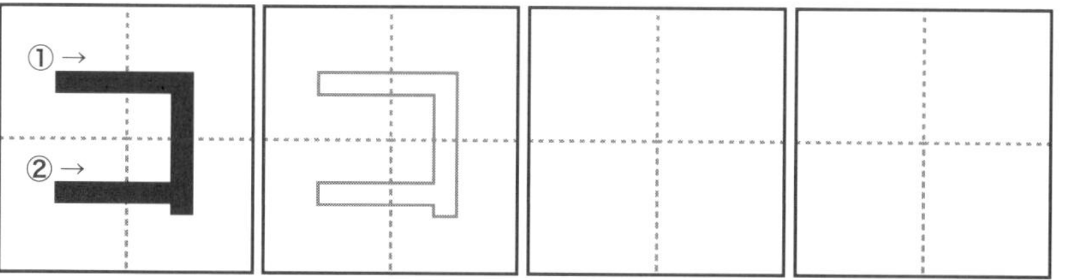

さむい

***sa**mui*

cold

If you've never been to Japan, you might not be aware that the country's northernmost main island, Hokkaido, is one of the coldest places on Earth, with winter temperatures falling well below freezing. Hokkaido is also the home of the あいぬ (Ainu), Japan's indigenous people. The word Ainu means "human."

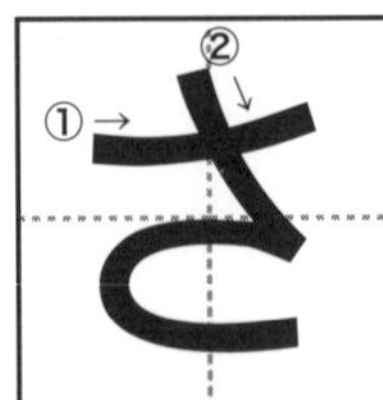

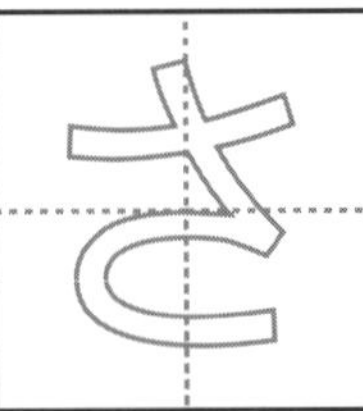

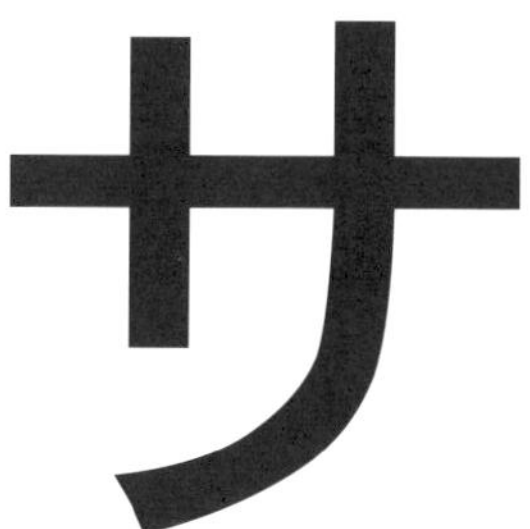

サラリーマン

***sa**rariiman*

salaryman
(businessman)

Pity the poor Japanese salaryman. His ぶちょう (bucho; boss) makes him work late into the night, he hasn't had a vacation in nearly 10 years, and now Mother Nature has blown his cover. Time to buy a new かつら (katsura; wig).

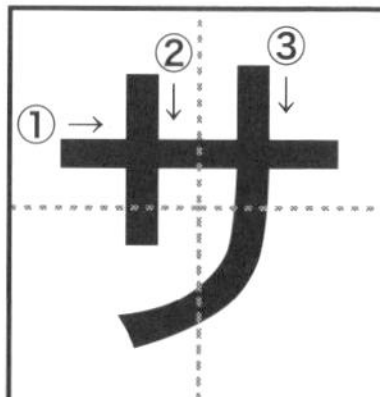

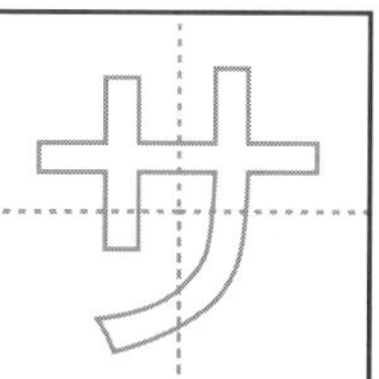

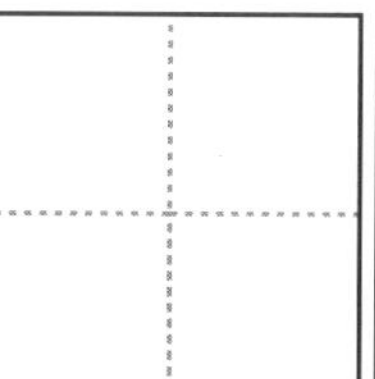

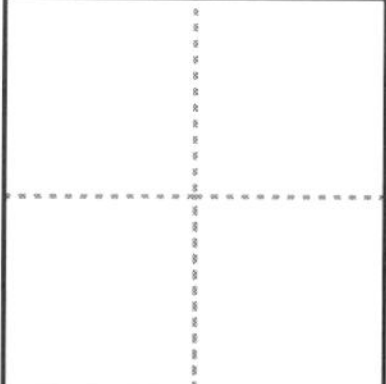

した

***shi*ta**

tongue

Sticking your tongue out at someone is rude in any culture. We have a feeling, though, that this kid has a problem keeping his tongue inside his big くち (kuchi; mouth).

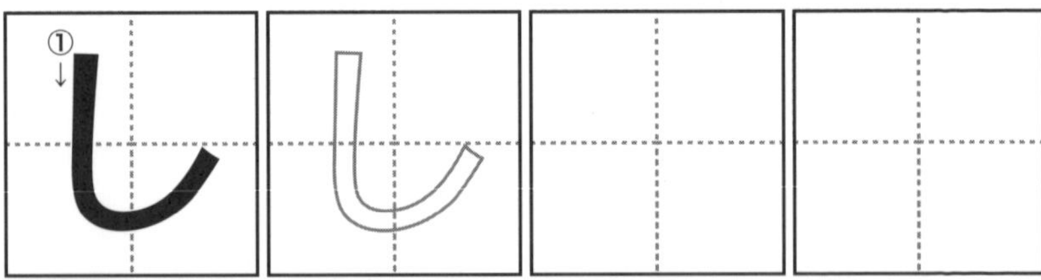

シール

***shii**ru*

seal

(sticker)

You'd think that playing with stickers would be a harmless activity. Not true, though, if おかあさん (okaasan; mom) just finished ぞうきんかけ (zokinkake; mopping the floor)!

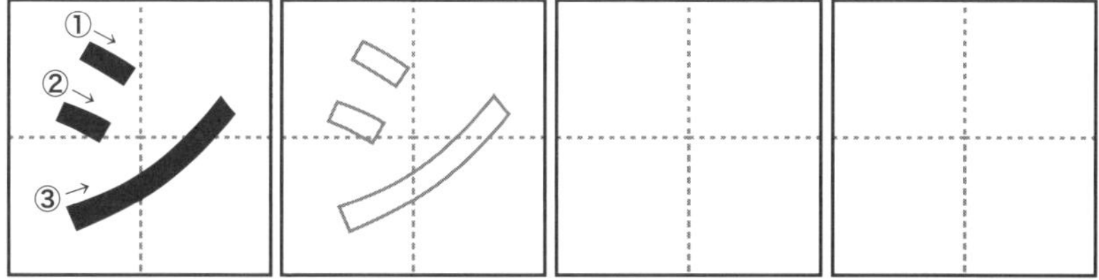

す

すもう
sumo
sumo
The ancient Japanese sport of sumo wrestling features some of the strongest—and largest—men in the world. One sumo superstar, the Hawaiian-born Konishiki, weighed more than 600 pounds at one point during his career!

①→ ②↓ す す

スイカ

***su**ika*

watermelon

Summertime is suika time in Japan, and kids flock to the beach to play スイカわり (suikawari), a game whose object is to split open a watermelon with a heavy stick while blindfolded. Similar to a Mexican pinata party ... but messier!

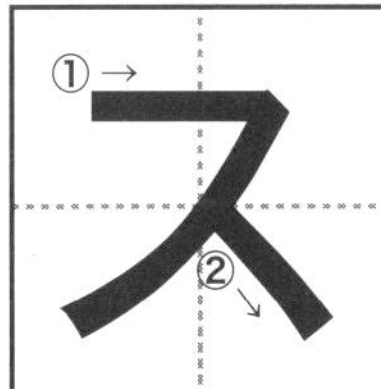

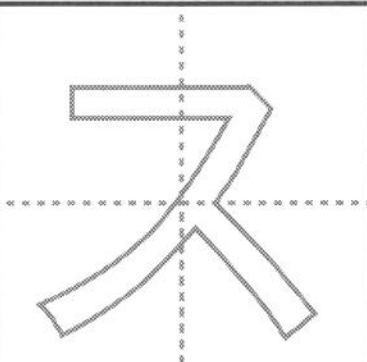

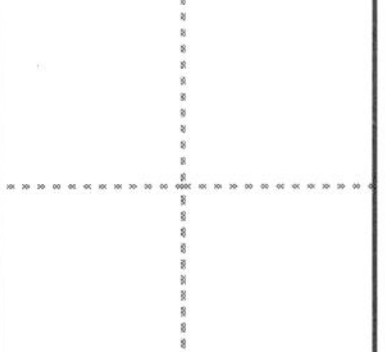

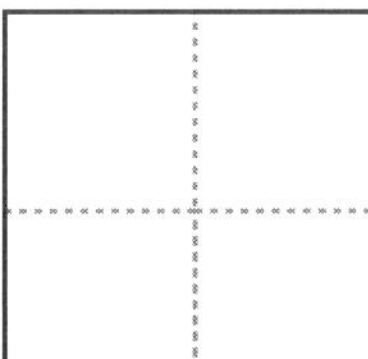

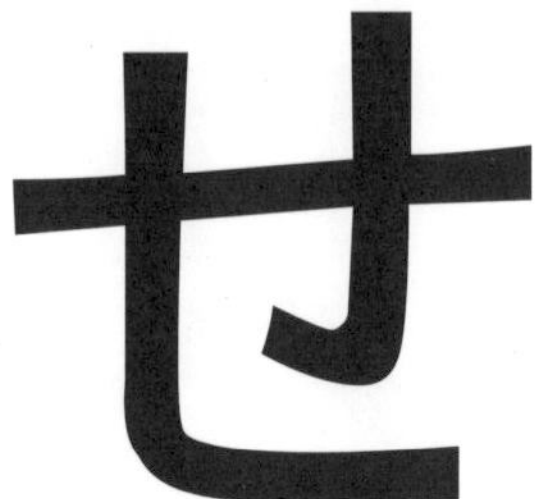

せいふく

***se*ifuku**

school uniform

By adding such things as designer scarves and ルーズソックス (ruuzu sokkusu; loose socks), girls have transformed their traditional school uniforms into ultra-chic fashion statements. せいふく is actually a shortened form of がくせいふく (gakuseifuku), which combines the words がくせい (gakusei; student) and ふく (fuku; clothes).

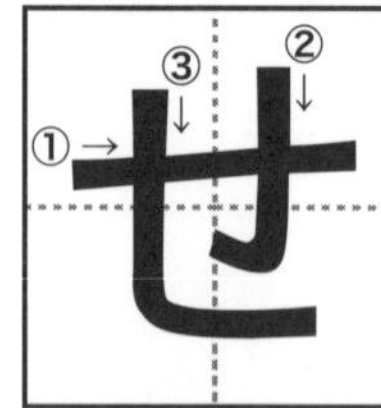

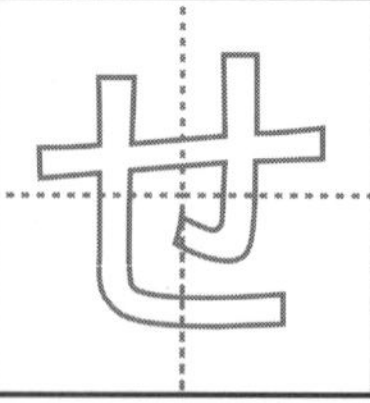

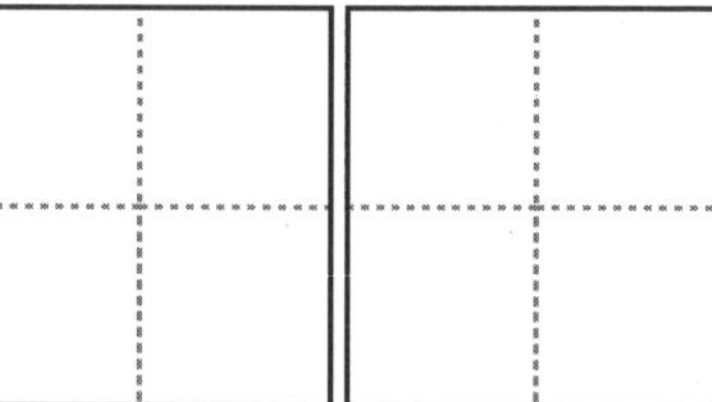

***se*etaa**

sweater

Another fashionable addition to the traditional school uniform is an おおきすぎる (okisugiru; oversized) sweater. Perfect for keeping the chill out during the bitterly cold ふゆ (fuyu; winter).

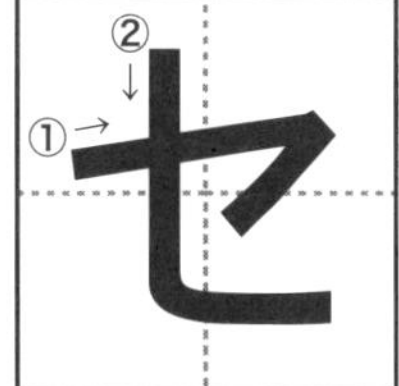

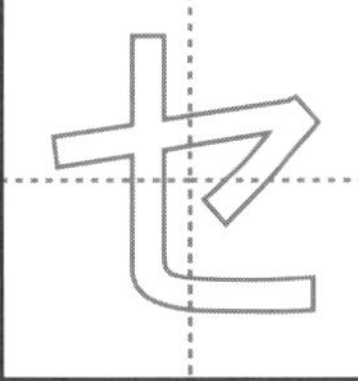

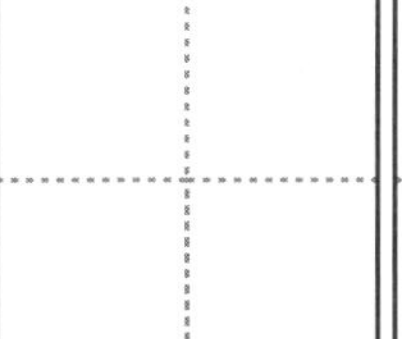

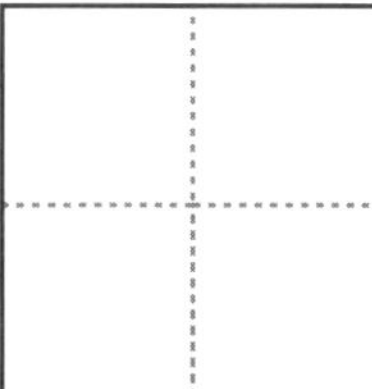

そつぎょう

sotsugyo

graduation

Ceremonies are held for graduating students at all levels of education in Japan, from preschool through college. However, equally important to the Japanese are にゅうがくしき (nyugakushiki), formal daylong events held when students enter school for the first time.

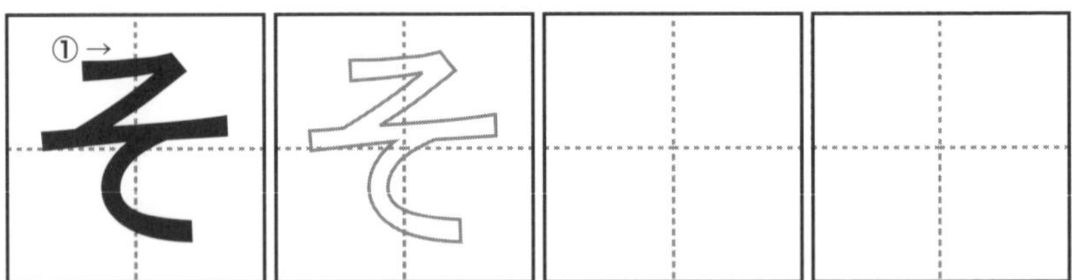

ソックス

***so*kkusu**

socks

Having a hole in your socks is nothing to be embarrassed about—unless you're inside a friend's いえ (ie; house) where shoes are not permitted. The traditional word for socks is くつした (kutsushita), which combines くつ (kutsu; shoes) and した (shita; below). The katakana form, however, is also widely used.

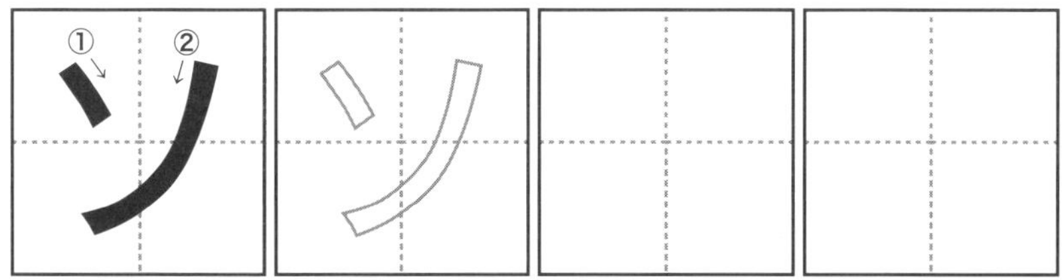

たからもの

***ta**karamono*

treasure

This word combines たから (takara; treasure) with もの (mono; things), to become "treasure things." Many other common nouns also end with もの. For instance, たべもの (tabemono; eating things, or food); のりもの (norimono; riding things, or vehicles); and わすれもの (wasuremono; lost/forgotten things).

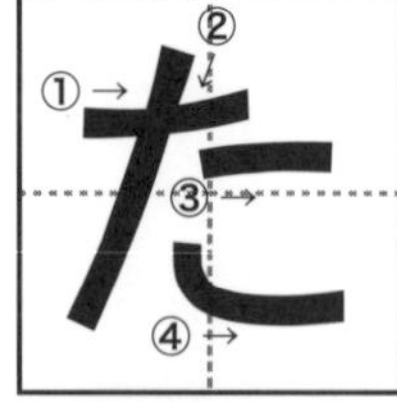

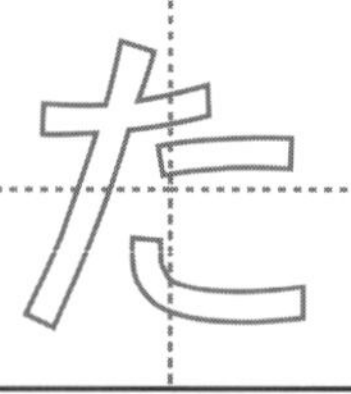

ターバン

***taa**ban*

turban

There are several species of へび (hebi; snakes) indigenous to Japan, but へびつかい (hebitsukai; snake charmers) hail from インド (Indo; India), of course.

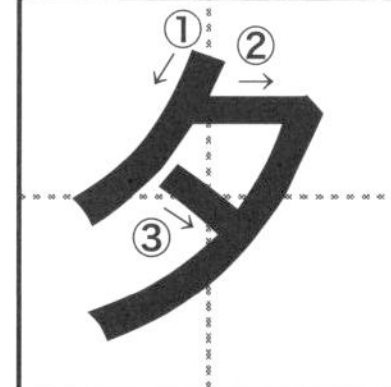

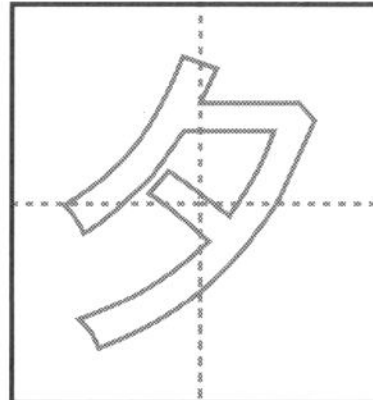

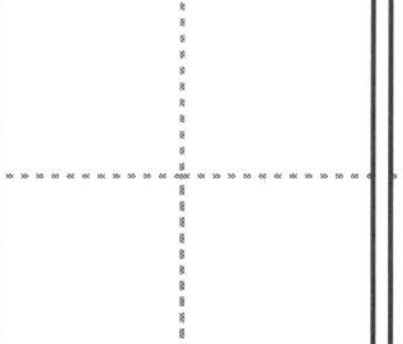

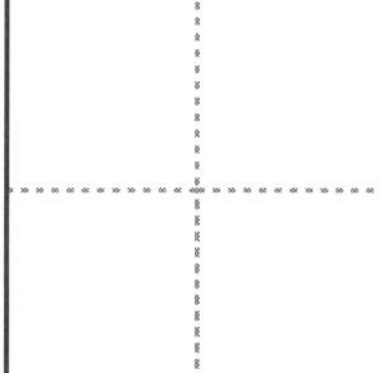

ち

ち

chi

blood

It may only be a little scratch, but try telling that to this おとこのこ (otoko no ko; boy). Judging by the look on his face, it's safe to assume he's just a wee bit squeamish when it comes to seeing his own blood. Ouch!

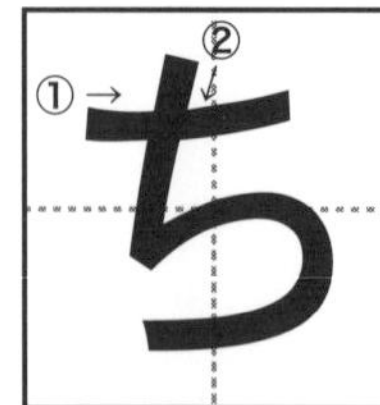

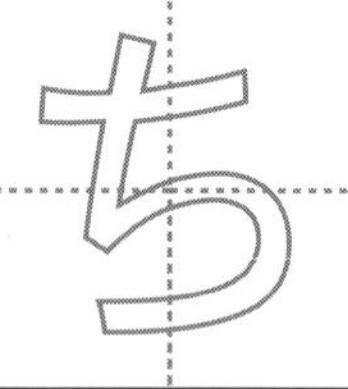

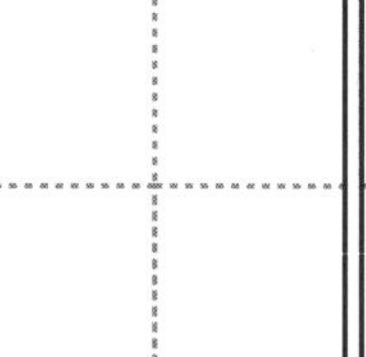

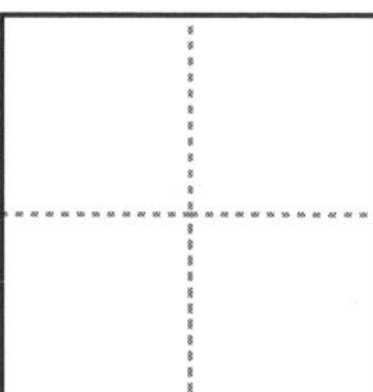

チアリーダー

***chi**ariidaa*

cheerleader

Gimme a ゴー! Gimme a チー! Gimme a ム! Gimme another ゴー! What does it spell? ゴーチームゴー (Go chiimu go; Go team, go)! OK, that was silly. But making up your own cheerleader chants using hiragana and katakana really is a great way to memorize the characters.

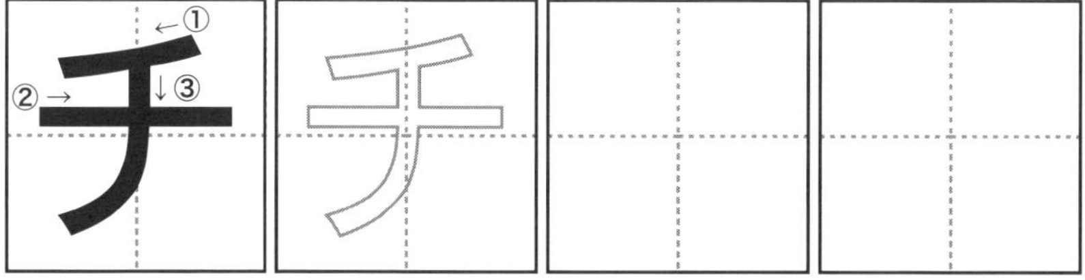

つき

***tsu*ki**

moon

The myth of the "the man in the moon" is well-known in North America and Europe. However, the Japanese take on this lunar legend is a bit different. Rather than the face of a man, they see the image of an うさぎ (usagi; rabbit) making もち (mochi; rice cakes).

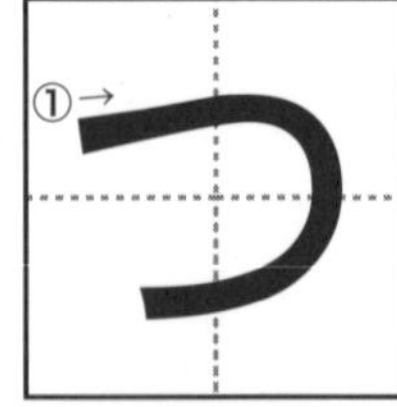

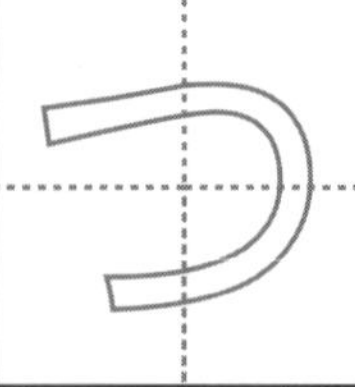

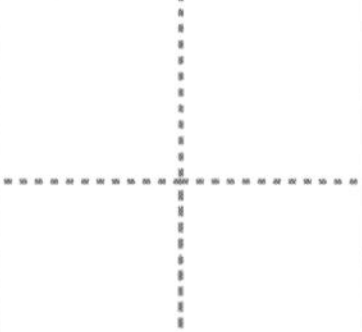

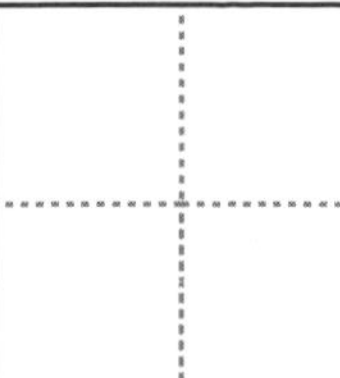

ツーショット

***tsuu**shotto*

two-shot

(photograph of a couple)

Many young Japanese couples enjoy taking photos together in what are called プリクラ (purikura; print clubs)—arcades with photograph vending machines that shoot and print images onto tiny stickers. The word プリクラ is a contraction of プリント (purinto; print) and クラブ (kurabu; club). はい、チーズ (Hai, chiizu; Say cheese)!

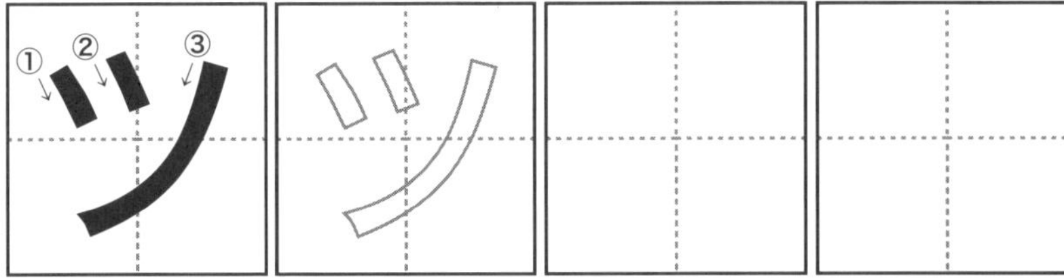

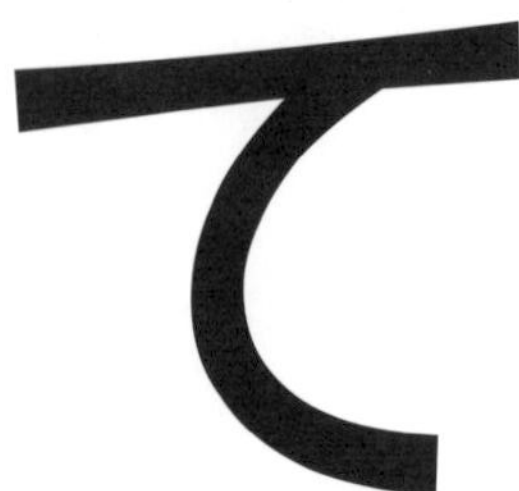

てじな

***te*jina**

magic

On its own, て (te) means "hand," and てじな quite literally translates as "sleight of hand." There are several ways to say "magician" in Japanese, including てじなし (tejinashi), which is also the word for "juggler," and マジシャン (majishan). And now watch as the magician pulls a rabbit out of her ぼうし (boshi; hat).

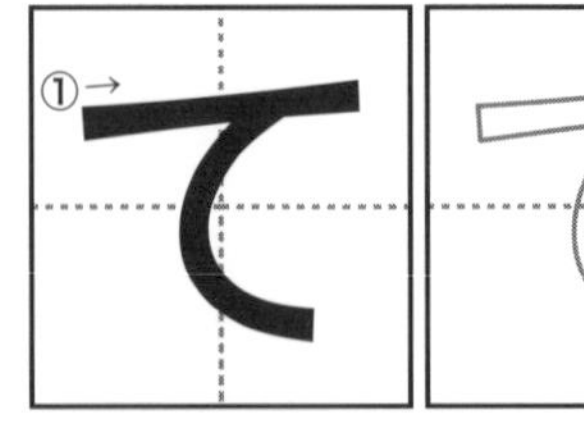

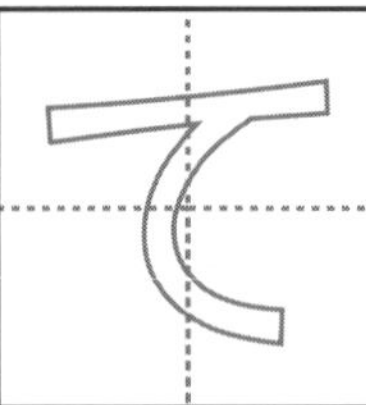

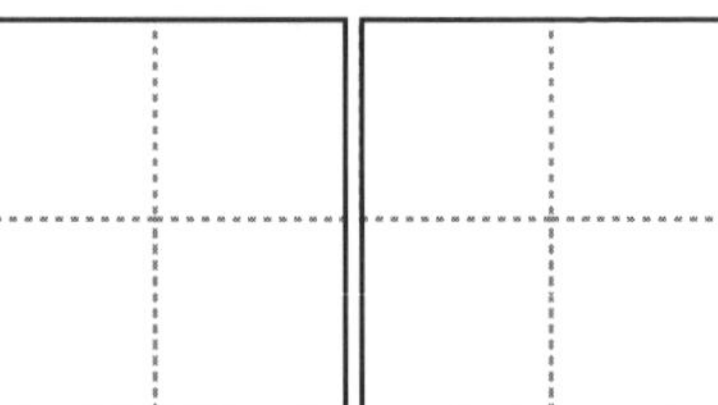

テスト

***te**suto*

test

The word "test" is a scary one in any language. Our friend here is worried he'll be denied the せんえん (senen; 1,000 yen) that mom has promised him if he gets a ごうかくてん (gokakuten; passing grade). He should have spent more time studying at the じゅく (juku; cram school).

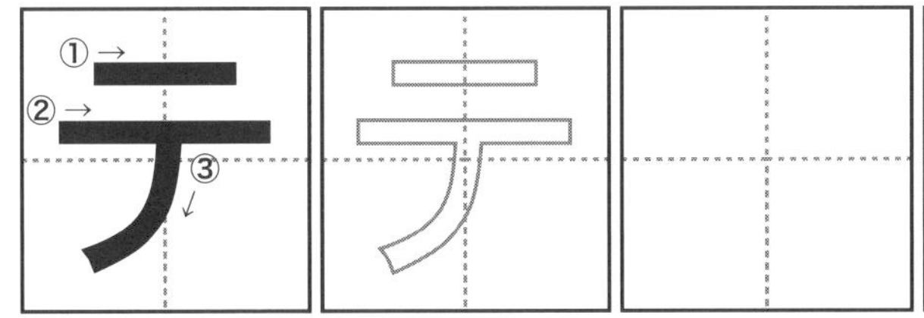

とんぼ

to**nbo**

dragonfly

Japan's first emperor is said to have once remarked that the shape of the country resembled that of a dragonfly, a symbol of playfulness and strength. To this day, Japanese fondly refer to their country as あきつしま (Akitsushima; The Dragonfly Islands).

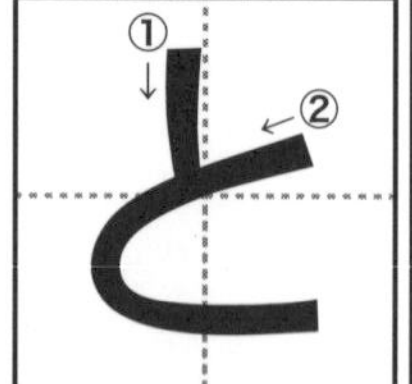

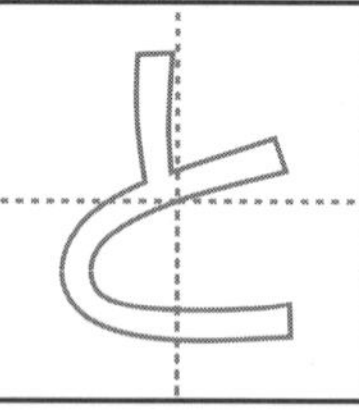

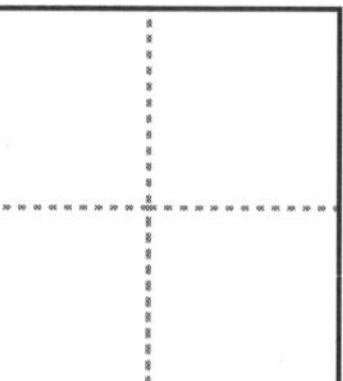

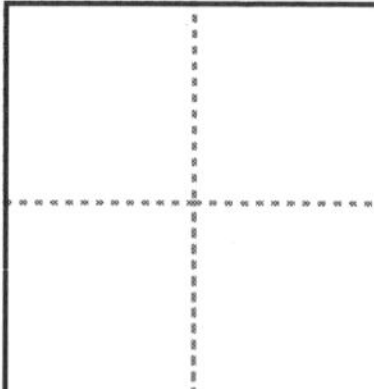

トイレット ペーパー

toirettopeipaa

toilet paper

Bathroom tissue is usually intended for serious "business," but this あかちゃん (akachan; baby) has found a whole new use for the stuff. Another word for toilet paper is おとしがみ (otoshigami).

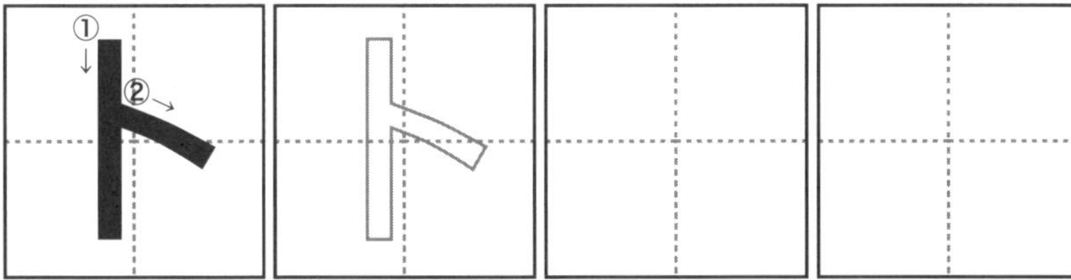

なきむし

***na*kimushi**

crybaby

Have you ever noticed that many アニメ(anime; Japanese cartoons) feature a main character who is always whining about something? Strange as it may seem, crybabies are often considered かわいい (kawaii; cute). Personally, we find them to be かわいそう (kawaiso; pathetic)!

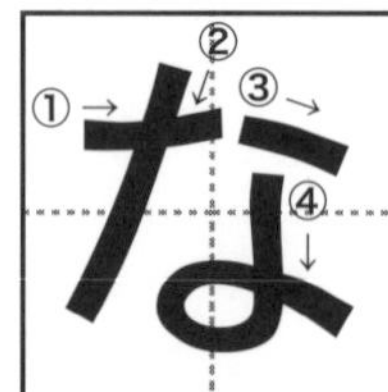

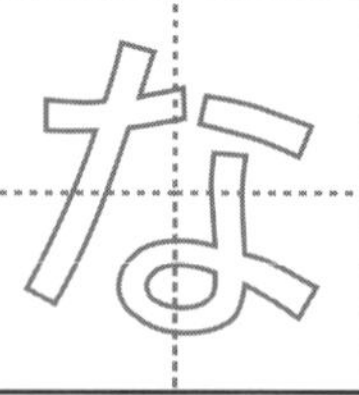

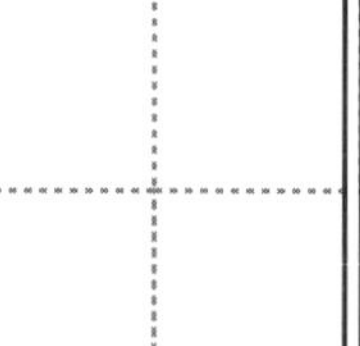

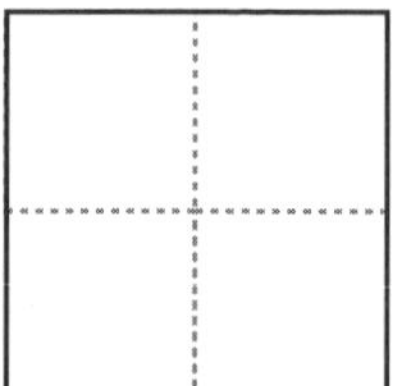

***naa*su**

nurse

"Trust me; this won't hurt a bit." How many times have you heard a nurse say that just before she sticks you with a foot-long needle? あぶないですよ (Abunai desu yo; Watch out)!

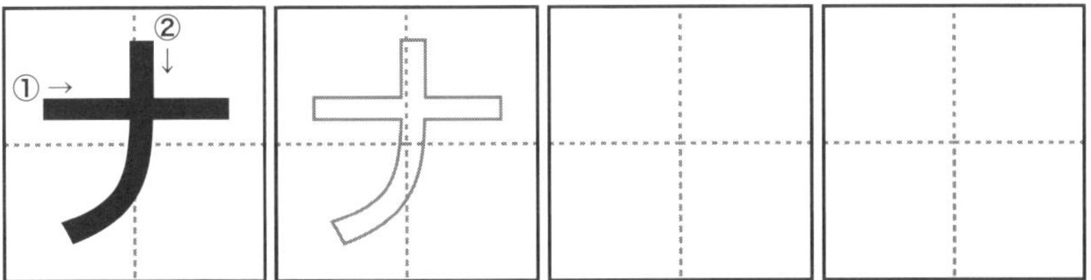

に

にんじゃ

ni**nja**

ninja

Countless movies have been made about the ninja and their service as secret assassins in feudal Japan. Truth, however, really is stranger than fiction. For instance, most of these stealth warriors were originally farmers—not fighters—and many of them were devout followers of the しんとう (Shinto) religion. Their full history, however, remains shrouded in mystery.

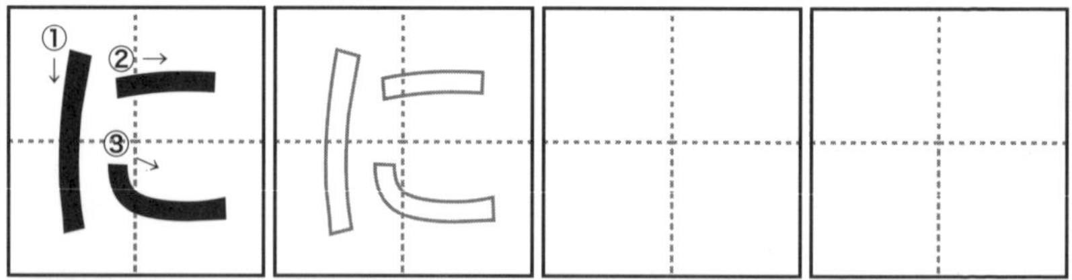

ニュース

***n*yuusu**

news

Watching Japanese news broadcasts on the テレビ (terebi; television) is another excellent way to improve your comprehension of the language. NHK, Japan's public broadcasting network, uses えいせいほうそう (eiseihoso; satellite broadcasts) to beam its newscasts to viewers throughout the world.

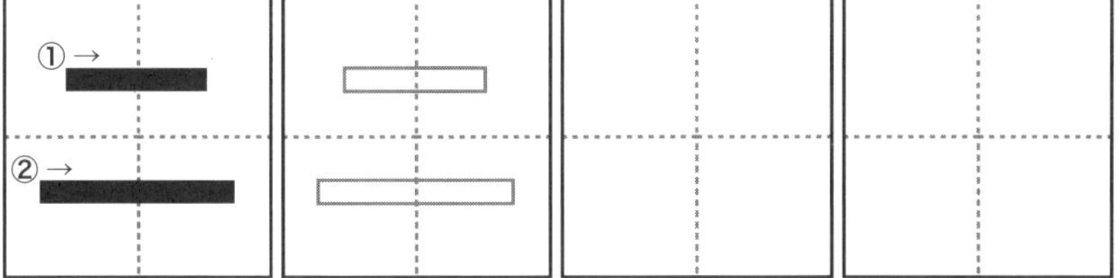

ぬれる

***nu**reru*

to get wet

If you've ever been in Japan during つゆ (tsuyu; the rainy season), you know the feeling of the poor guy pictured here. This miserable meteorological period usually begins in late May and continues well into July, when temperatures begin to soar and things get really むしあつい (mushiatsui; hot and humid).

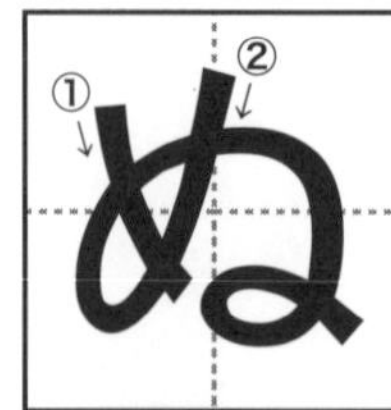

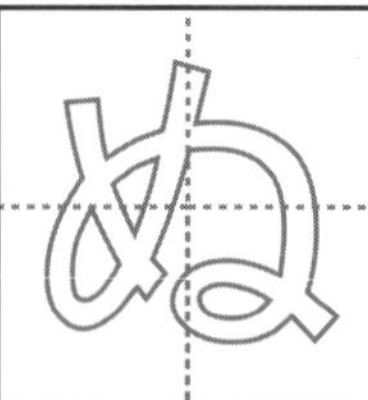

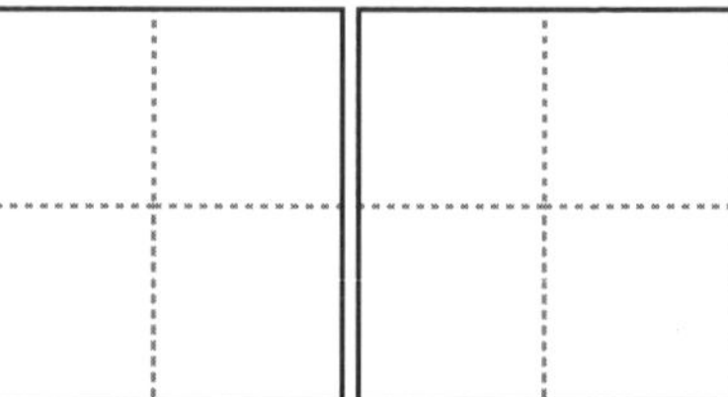

ヌンチャク

***nu**nchaku*

nunchaku

This well-known weapon is said to have originated in ancient Okinawa, a large island that lies about halfway between Japan (of which Okinawa is now a part) and Taiwan. Martial-arts historians believe the first nunchaku were used not as weapons but rather as some sort of farming tool. Another word for nunchaku is そせつこん (sosetsukon), though it is not as common.

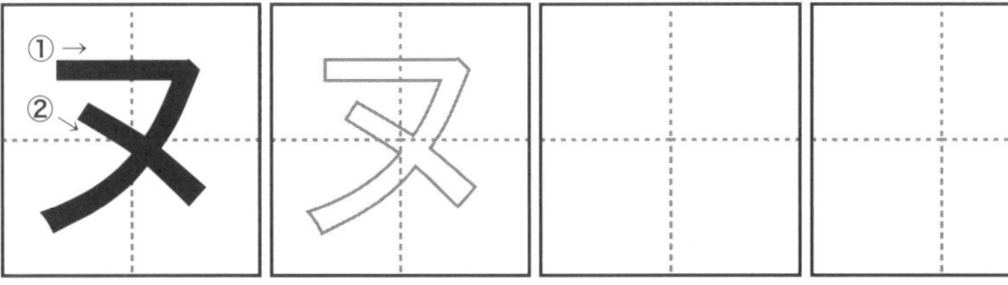

ねこ

***ne**ko*

cat

Nearly 8 million of Japan's cramped homes still manage to make room for pet cats. Ceramic feline figurines called まねきねこ (manekineko; beckoning cat) are kept as good-luck charms by nearly every business owner in the land. And Hello Kitty is a national icon. Make no doubt about it: Japan is the cat's meow.

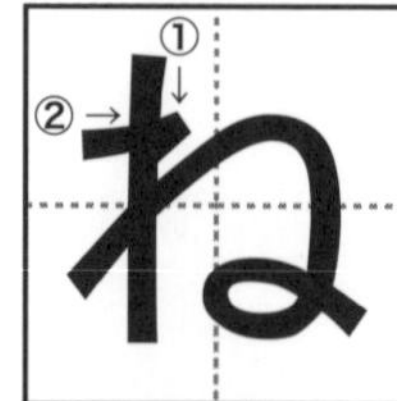

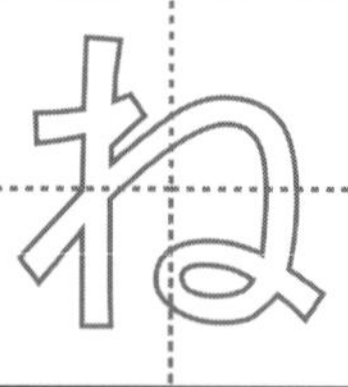

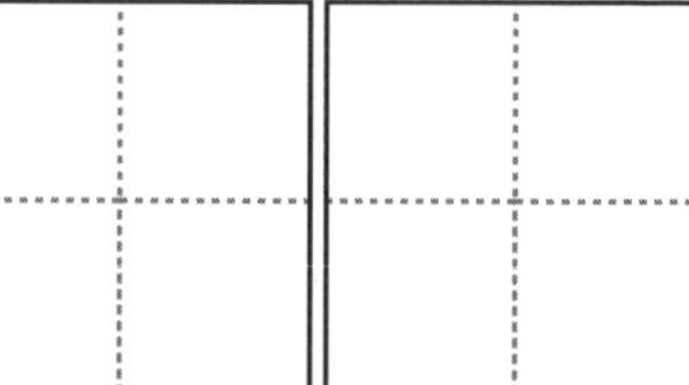

ネクタイ

***ne*kutai**

necktie

In nearly every Japanese オフィス (ofuisu; office), male employees are required to wear スーツ (suutsu; suits) and neckties. Dad may be a traditionalist, but we think the little guy has the right idea.

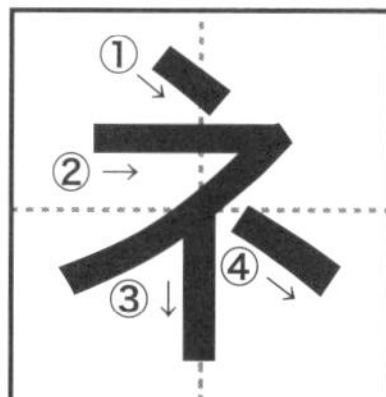

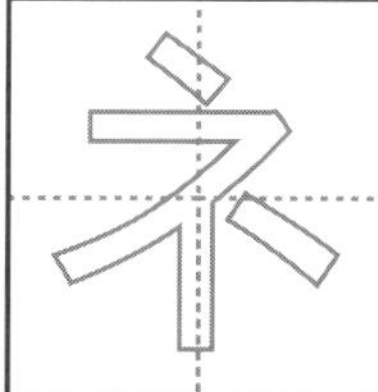

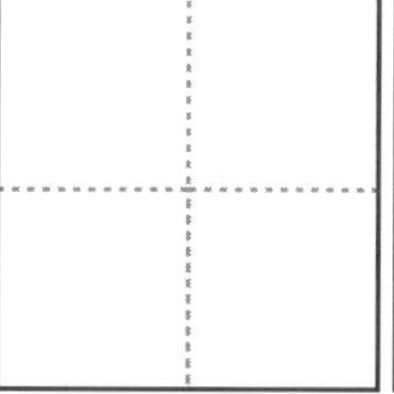

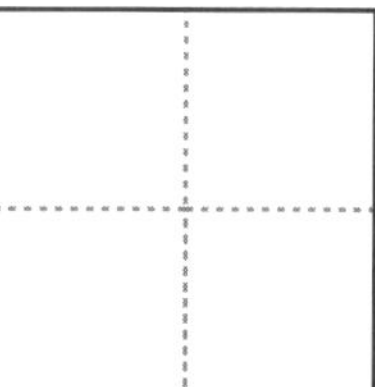

のっぺらぼう

nopperabo

faceless female ghost

This expressionless apparition is one of Japan's most famous おばけ (obake; monsters). Legend has it that she haunts men who have harmed women. Many Japanese horror stories take place in summer during おぼん (obon; the Lantern Festival), when ghosts are said to return to their ancestral homes.

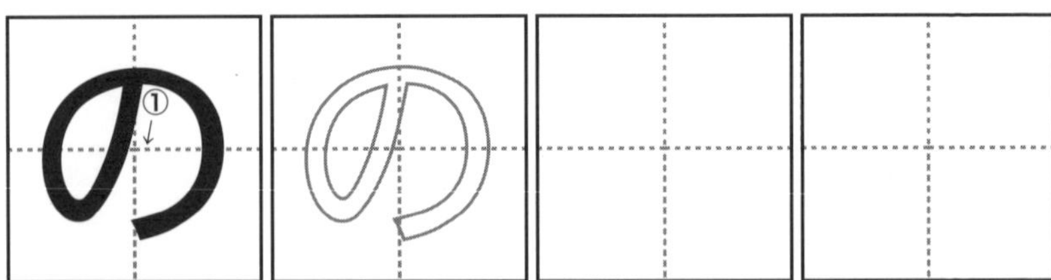

ノック

***no**kku*

knock

Many people in Japan keep the doors to their homes unlocked. So when a visitor arrives, rather than knocking, he or she will simply open the door and proclaim ごめんください (gomen kudasai), which means "Excuse me," "I'm here" or "May I come in?"

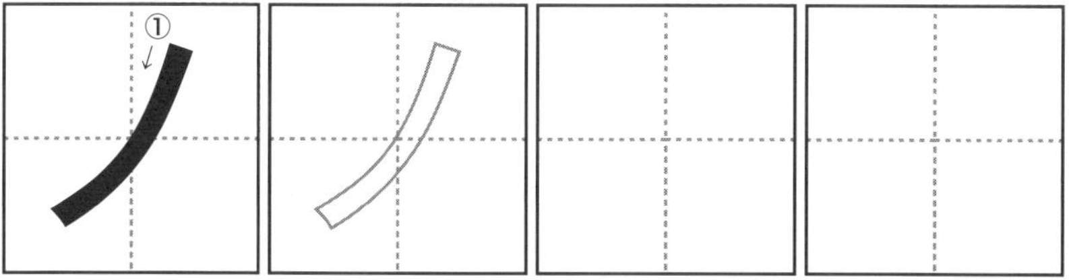

はな

***ha*na**

flower

Although Japan does not have an official national flower, the さくら (sakura; cherry blossom) certainly symbolizes the country. When the cherry trees are in full bloom (usually in late March), huge crowds gather in local parks for はなみ (hanami; flower viewing) parties. The きく (kiku; chrysanthemum) is also a Japanese favorite, and is used in the Imperial Family's crest.

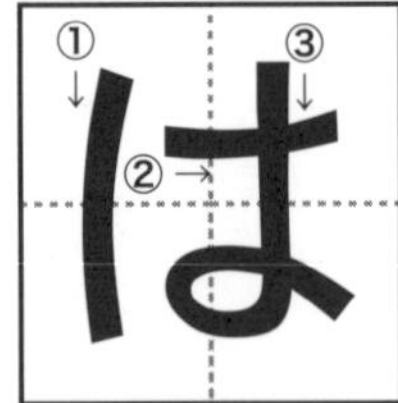

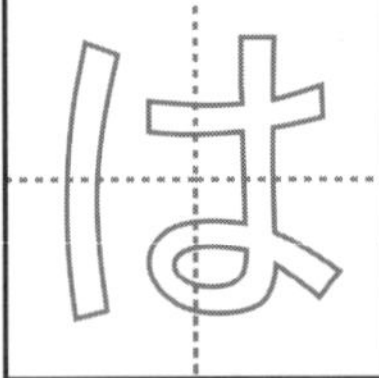

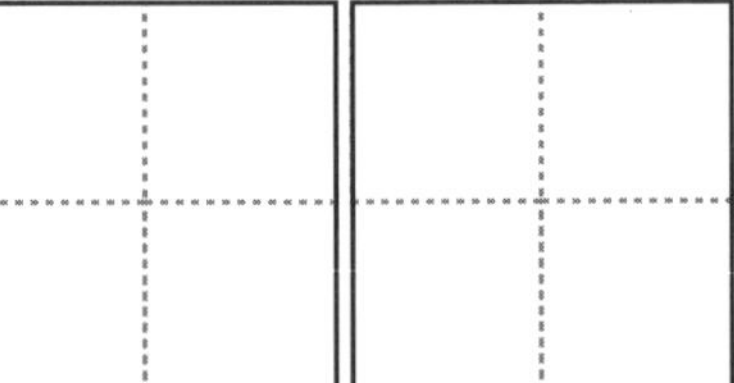

ハンバーガー

hanbaagaa

hamburger

Western-style restaurants abound in Japan, and hamburgers are always available. However, take care when placing your order. With the bun, it's a ハンバーガー (hanbaagaa); without the bun, it's called ハンバーグ (hanbaagu). Either way, we like it topped with チーズ (chiizu; cheese).

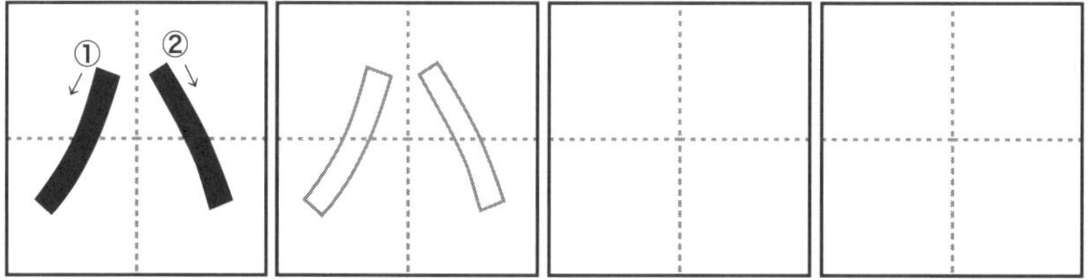

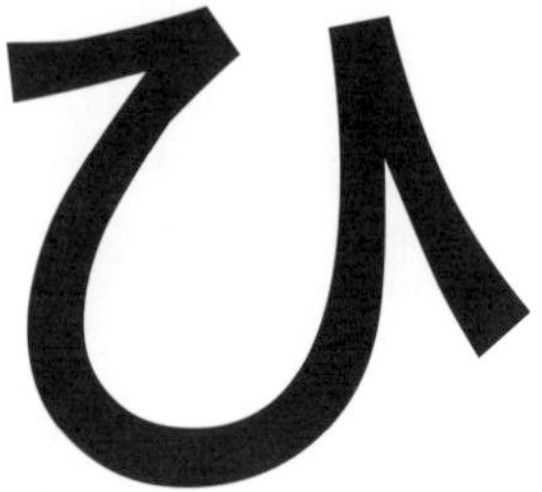

ひとめぼれ

***hi**tomebore*

love at first sight

It's a familiar scene: Boy sees girl, boy falls head-over-heels for girl, girl goes to the prom with the captain of the からて (karate) team instead. To paraphrase the French, しょうがない (shoganai; c'est la vie).

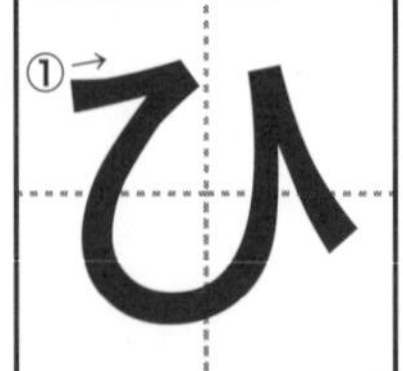

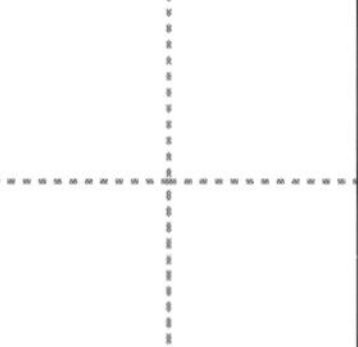

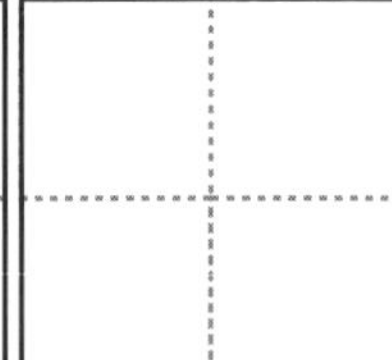

ヒーロー

***hii**roo*

superhero

Superheroes with such names as ウルトラマン (Urutoraman; Ultraman) and スペクトルマン (Supekutoruman; Spectreman) have long been the stars of Japanese television programs for young boys. Alas, most of these young hero-worshipers grow up to be what the Japanese call a サラリーマン (sarariiman; salaryman, or company employee) instead.

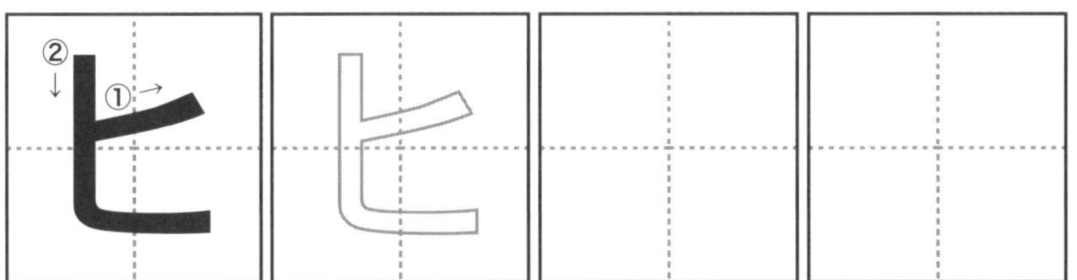

***fu**kutsu*

stomachache

Our friend here seems to be in a bit of pain. Must have been that bad すし (sushi) he had for lunch. Time to head to the local びょういん (byoin; hospital).

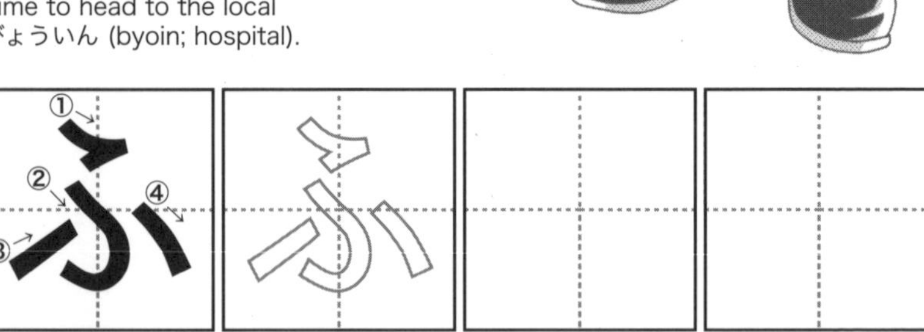

フクロウ

***fu**kuro*

owl

Is it possible to learn the secrets of the universe from a wise old owl? Perhaps. But you will probably have to adjust your schedule, as this particular やちょう (yacho; nocturnal bird) only teaches night classes.

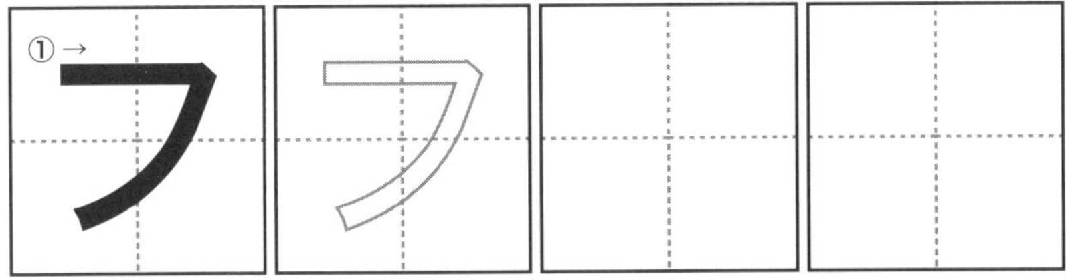

へいあんじだい

***he**ianjidai*

The Heian Period

This period (794-1185) in Japanese history was marked by an unprecedented political stability that fostered the cultural refinement, or "Japanization," of the land. Buddhism began to flourish, and literary and artistic masterpieces were created. However, the period also saw the rise of the powerful samurai (さむらい) class of professional soldiers, whose fierce loyalty to regional warlords ultimately spelled the end for Heian tranquility.

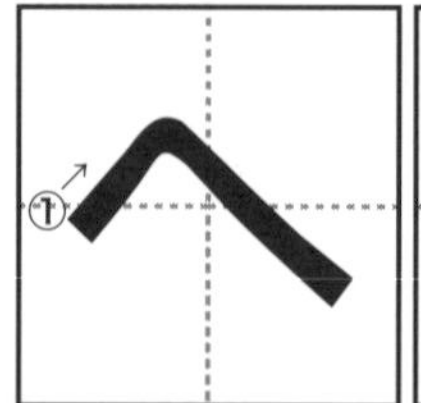

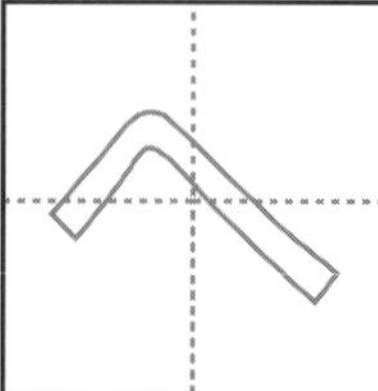

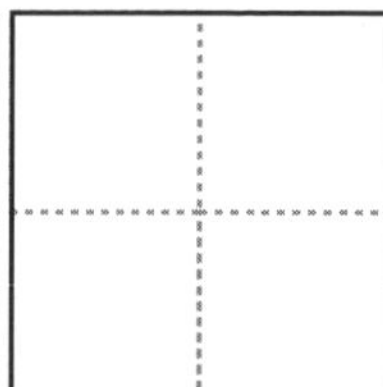

ヘルスメーター

***he**rusumeetaa*

health meter

(bathroom scale)

No matter how petite she really is, this young lady feels like a こぶた (kobuta; little pig). And the numbers don't lie. She's gained 2 ounces—that's right, 2 ounces!—since she last month.

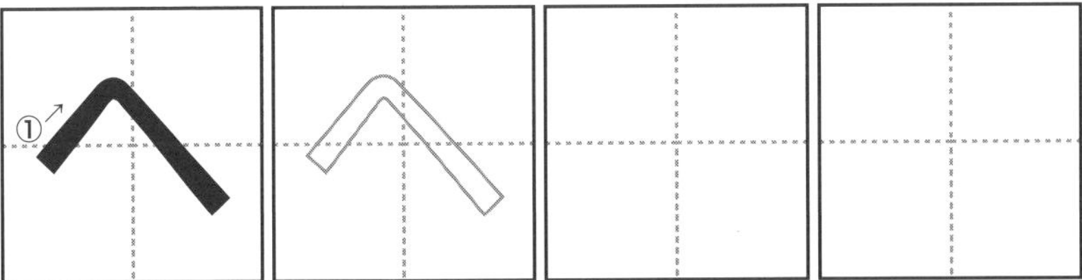

ほし

***ho*shi**

star

For the most part, people in Japan see the same "pictures" in the night skies as do North Americans and Europeans. But their names for many せいざ (seiza; constellations) are distinctly Japanese. For example, Lyra, the lyre, is called こと (koto), the name of a traditional Japanese stringed instrument. Just remember that when you wish upon a star, you can do so in any language.

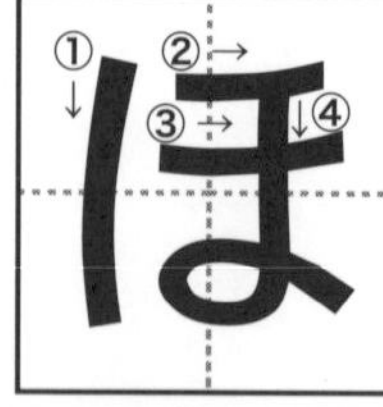

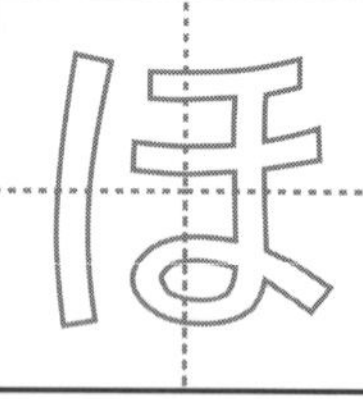

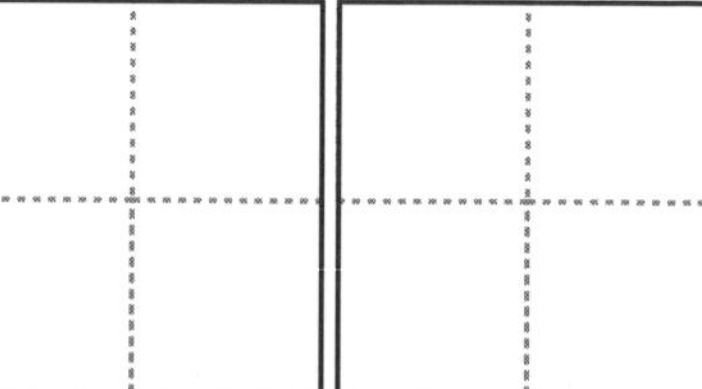

ホラーえいが

***ho**raaeiga*

horror movie

The first part of this word, ホラー (horaa), is how the Japanese pronounce the English word "horror." The second part, えいが (eiga), means "movie." The Japanese love horror movies, especially those about もののけ (mononoke; vengeful ghosts).

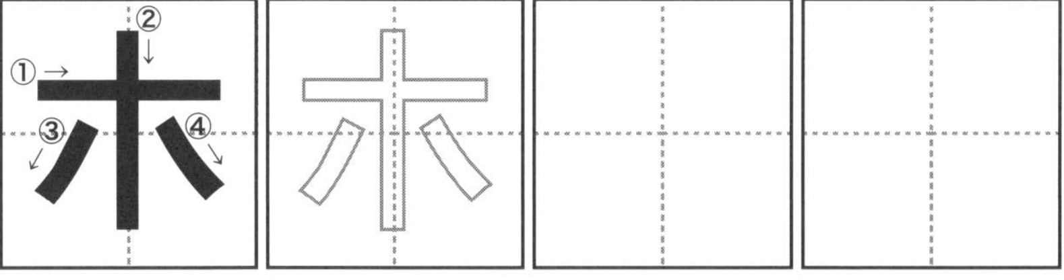

まり

***ma*ri**

ball

This is the traditional word for ball, although the katakana ボール (which, when pronounced, sounds like "ball") is quite common. The girl pictured here is dressed in a ゆかた (yukata; summer kimino) and ぞうり (zori, Japanese sandals).

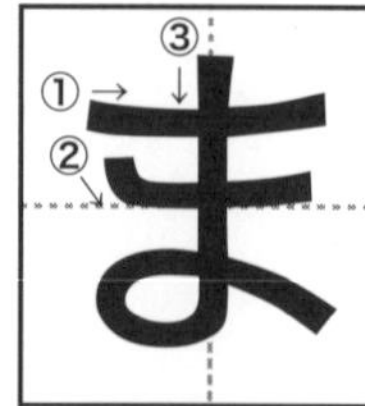

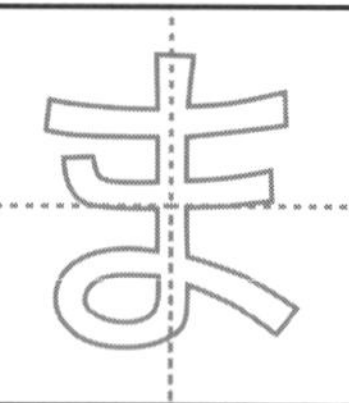

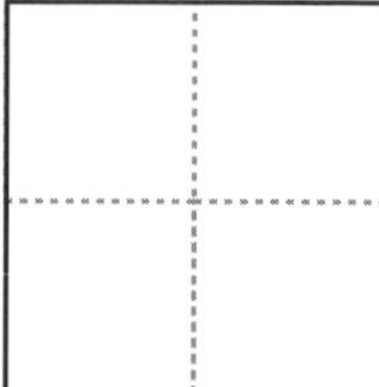

マフラー

***ma*furaa**

muffler

Designer mufflers are very popular with じょがくせい (jogakusei; schoolgirls), and many boys also wear them. Favorite brands include バーバリー (Baabarii; Burberry) and エルメス (Erumesu; Hermes).

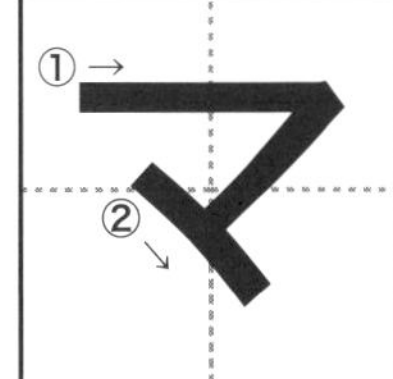

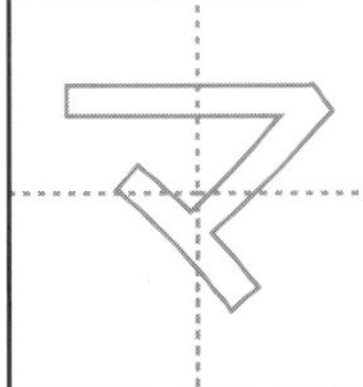

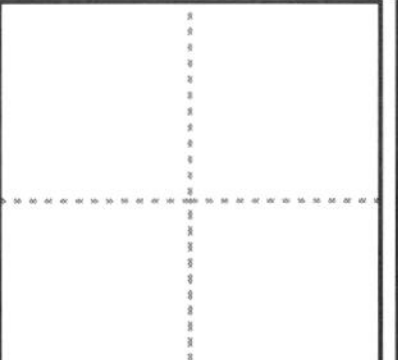

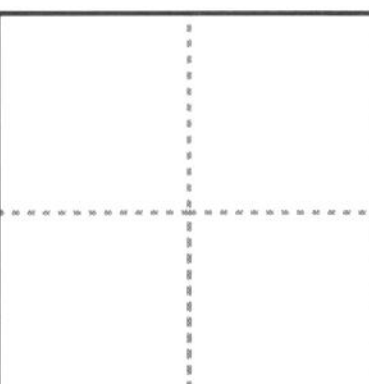

***mi*ko**

shrine maiden

In ancient times, miko were young women believed to be endowed with mystical powers that allowed them to divine messages from the かみ (kami; gods). Modern じんぐう (jingu; Shinto shrines) still employ miko, who today serve primarily as caretakers and assistants to the しんかん (shinkan; Shinto priests).

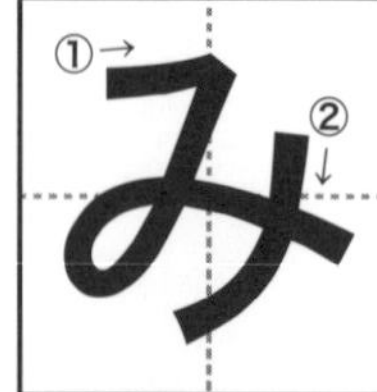

ミュージック

***m**yuujikku*

music

Japan has music for all tastes, ranging from easy-listening えんか (enka; love ballads) to J一ポップス (J-poppusu; Japanese pop) to ヴィジュアルロック (buijyuarurokku; literally, "visual rock," or hard rock). The traditional word for music is おんがく (ongaku).

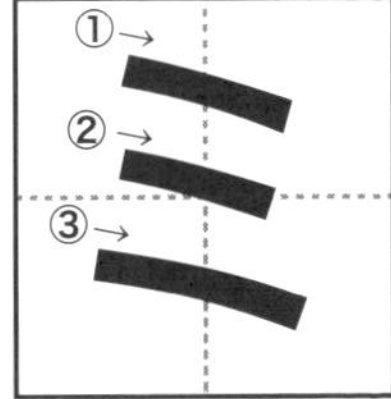

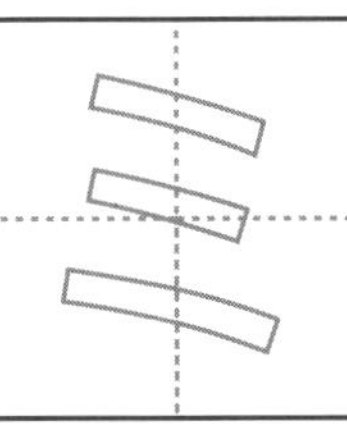

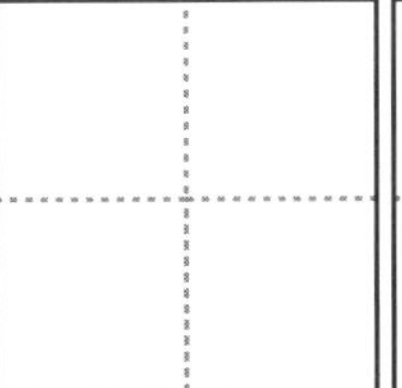

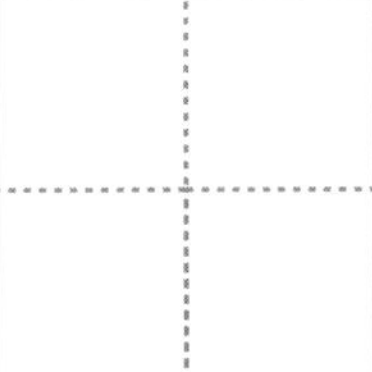

むきりょく

***mu**kiryoku*

lethargic

Hey, don't give up yet! If you've been studying them つぎつぎ (tsugitsugi; one by one), you've already learned more than half the kana in this book! がんばってください (Ganbatte kudasai; Keep going, you can do it)!

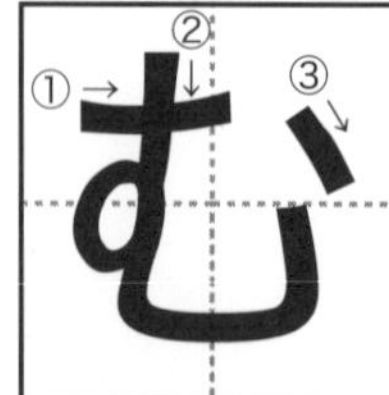

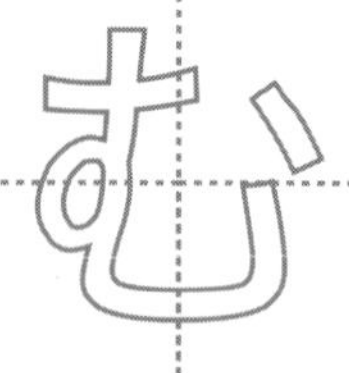

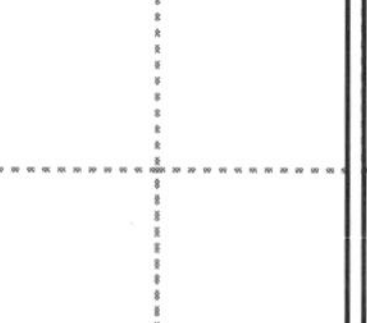

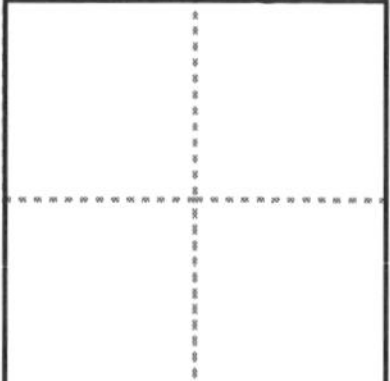

ムササビ

***mu*sasabi**

flying squirrel

With a wingspan of about 18 inches, the Japanese giant flying squirrel is among the largest of its kind in the world. The musasabi is a nocturnal animal and glides from one き (ki; tree) to another at a slow, graceful pace.

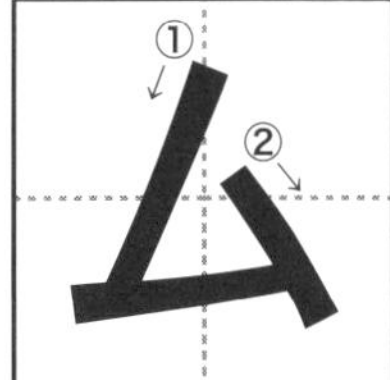

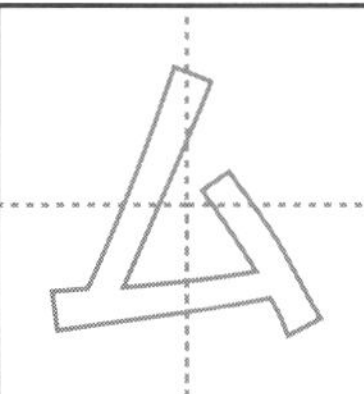

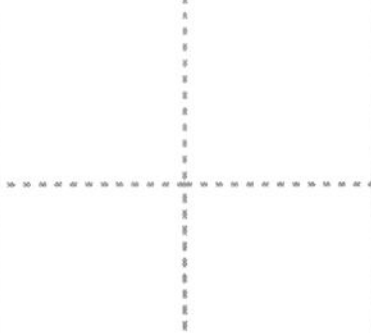

めざましどけい

***me**zamashidokei*

alarm clock

The first part of this word, めざまし, comes from the verb めざめる (mezameru), which means "to wake." The ending, どけい, is an alternate way of pronouncing とけい (tokei), the generic word for "clock." We'll leave it to you to figure out what the word スヌーズボタン (sunuuzu botan) means.

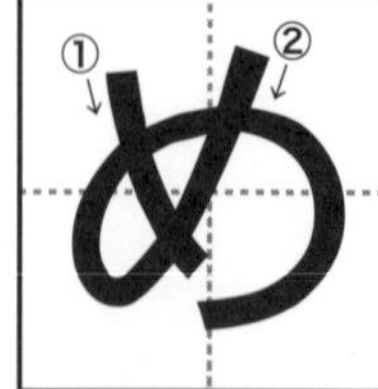

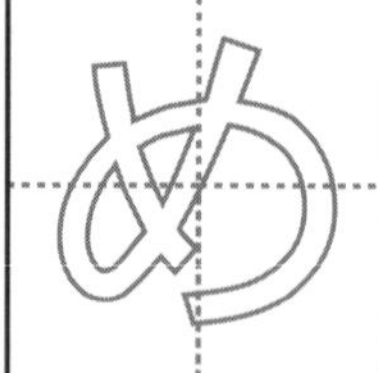

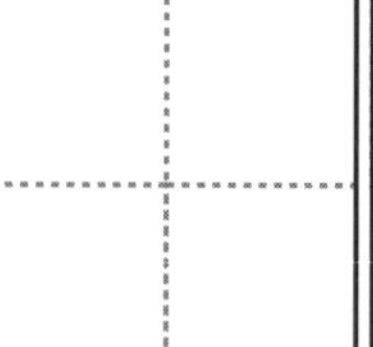

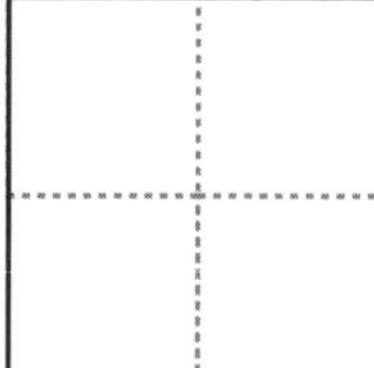

メガホン

***me**gahon*

megaphone

Students in Japan really know how to show their とうし (toshi; fighting spirit). At sporting events, they sing school songs, bang drums, blow horns and wave flags the entire time. Naturally, megaphones are an indispensable part of the cheering section's equipment.

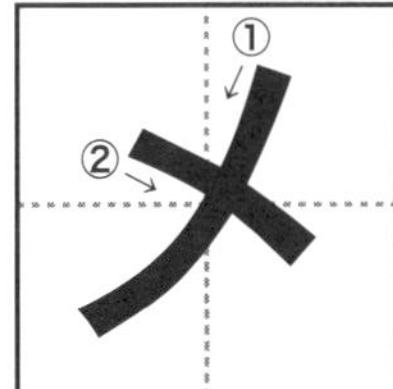

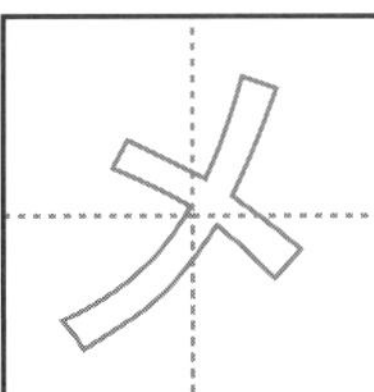

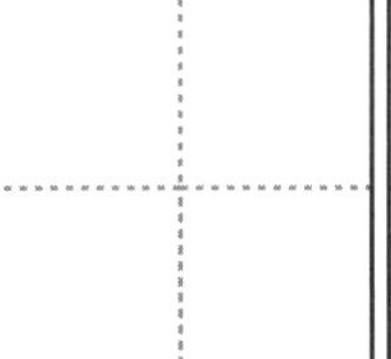

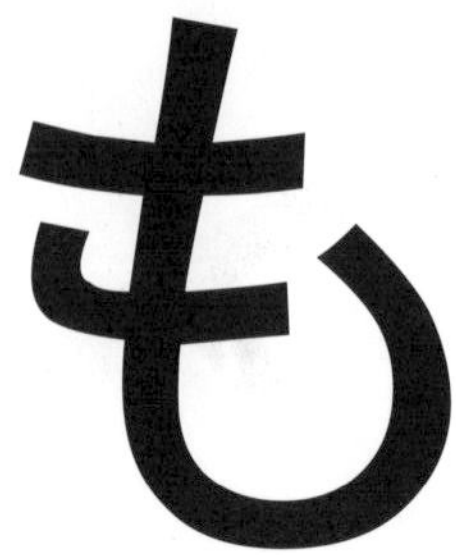

もぐら

***mo*gura**

mole

Because they like to dig late at night or early in the morning, moles often are the mascots of road crews in Japan. The sign behind these two rascals reads (in kanji), こうじちゅう (kojichu; under construction), and they are wearing Japanese-style hard hats.

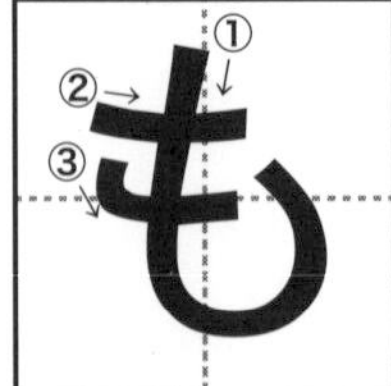

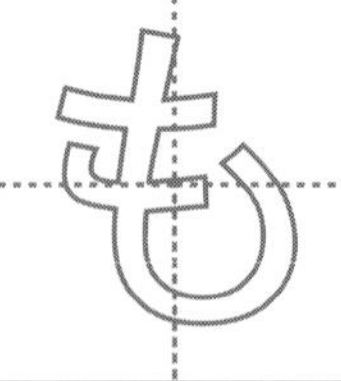

モップ

***mo**ppu*

mop

Man's best friend is also a boy's best buddy. The young owner of this shaggy いぬ (inu; dog) knows his pal could use a ヘアーカット(heaakatto; haircut), but he loves the mop top just the same.

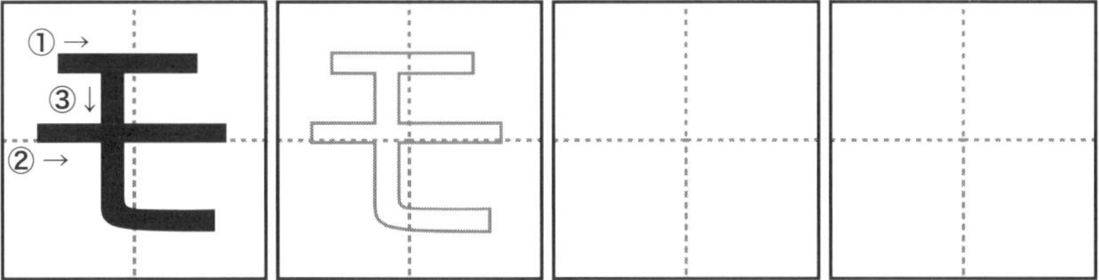

やじるし

***ya**jirushi*

direction arrow

Japanese ひょうしき (hyoshiki; road signs) are among the most confusing in the world, primarily because the streets in most cities crisscross one another in a way that defies logic. It's enough to make one's head spin.

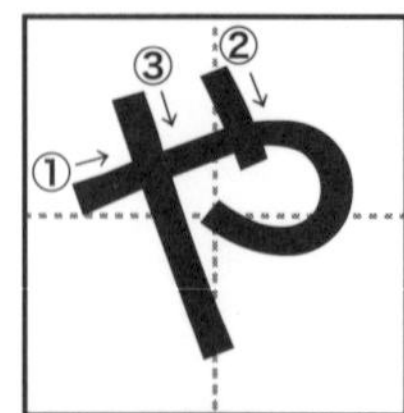

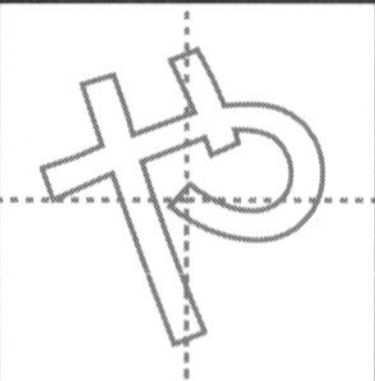

ヤカン

***ya**kan*

kettle

Here is a word that can be written in either katakana or hiragana. Literally, ヤカン (or やかん) means "medicine pot." Chicken スープ (supu; soup), anyone?

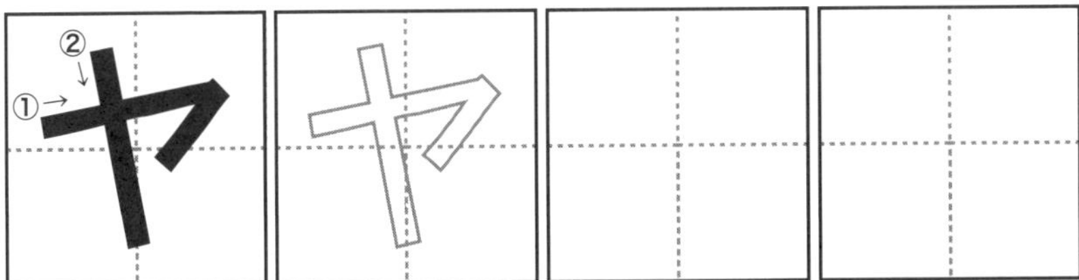

ゆきだるま

***yu*kidaruma**

snowman

The shape of a snowman somewhat resembles that of a Japanese だるま (daruma; dharma doll), hence the name ゆきだるま, with ゆき (yuki) being the word for snow. Dharma dolls are given as good luck charms to students, politicians, businesspeople and others who are trying to achieve difficult goals.

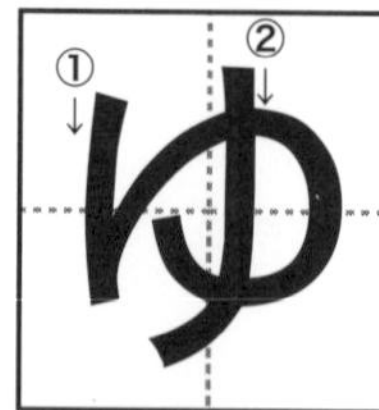

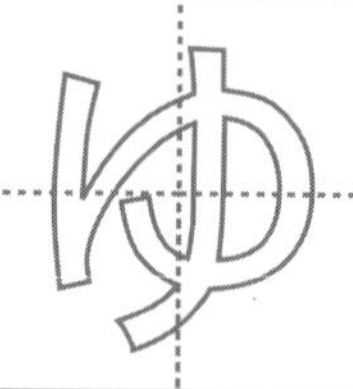

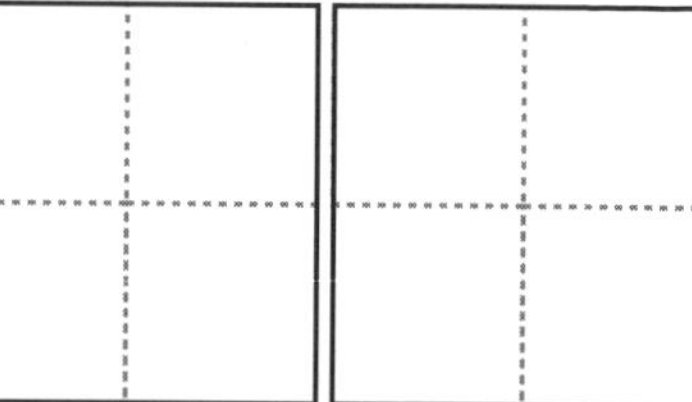

ユーフォ

yuufuo

UFO

UFO sightings are common in Japan, though most of them take place not in the sky but inside supermarkets. That's where conspiracy theorists can find UFO-brand instant やきそば (yakisoba; stir-fried noodles), which is sold in a flying saucer-shaped dish. Alien not included.

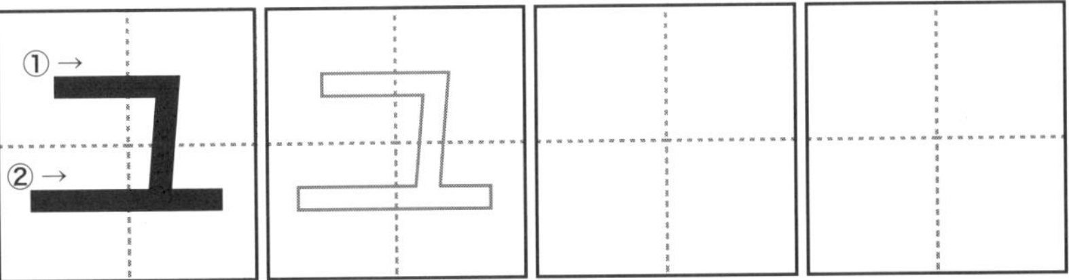

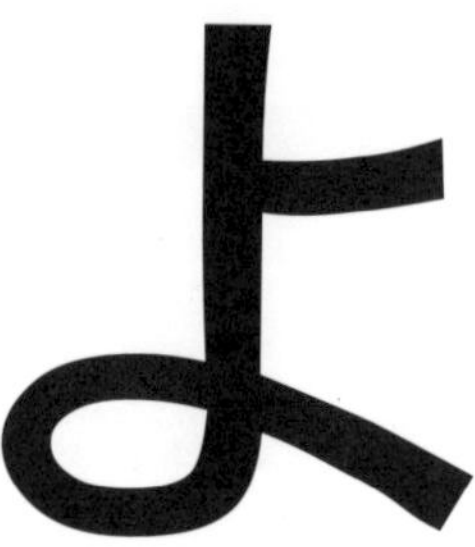

ようせい

***yo*sei**

fairy

Water sprites and other types of fairies hold a prominent place in Japanese みんぞくがく (minzokugaku; folklore). Especially beloved are the rascally water demons called かっぱ (kappa). These creatures are said to love cucumbers, which is why cucumber-filled sushi rolls are called かっぱまき (kappamaki; kappa rolls).

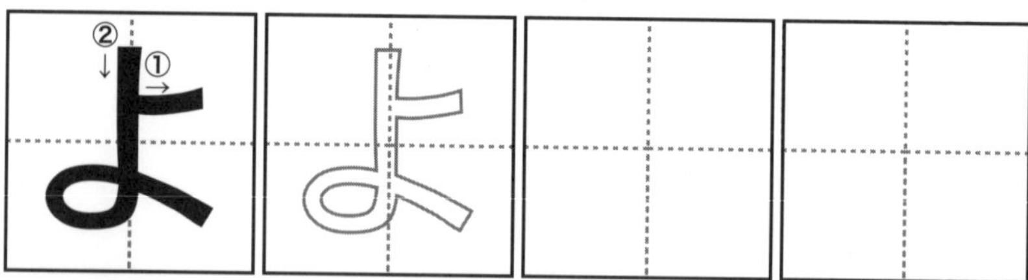

*yo*oyoo

yo-yo

Children throughout the world have been playing with these simple toys for more than 2,500 years. The name itself comes from Tagalog, the native language of the Philippines, and means "come come" or "come back." In Japan, the numeral four is pronounced "yon" (よん), which sounds "yo," and thus the fourth day of the fourth month (April 4, or "yon-yon") is unofficially recognized by toy makers as Yo-Yo Day.

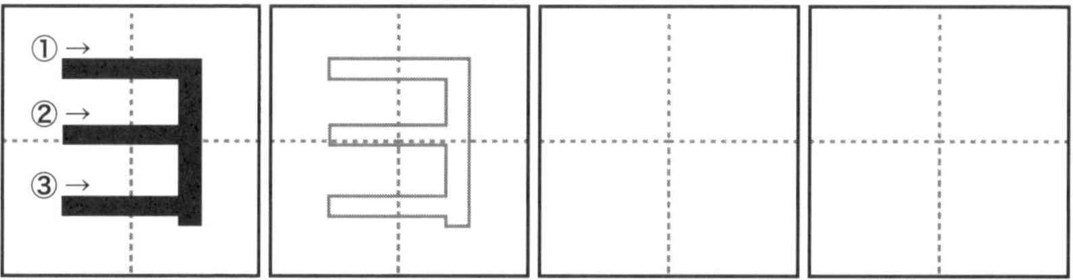

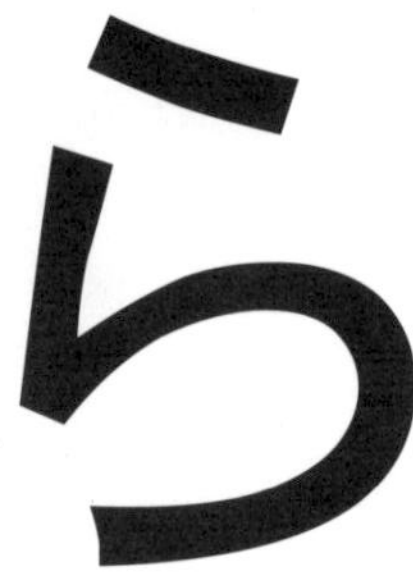

らいう

raiu

thunderstorm

The odds of being struck by らいこう (raiko; lightning) are 700,000 to 1. The odds that you've already memorized the first 72 kana in this ほん (hon; book) are 3 to 1. We like your chances.

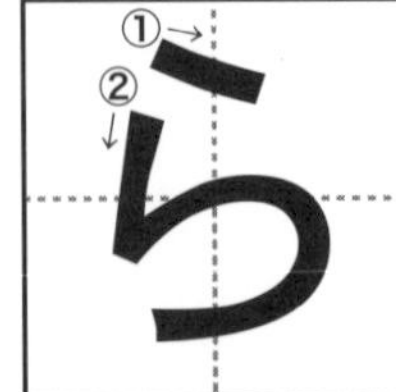

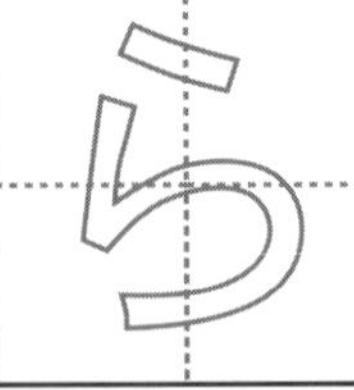

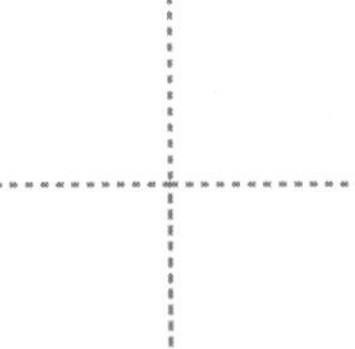

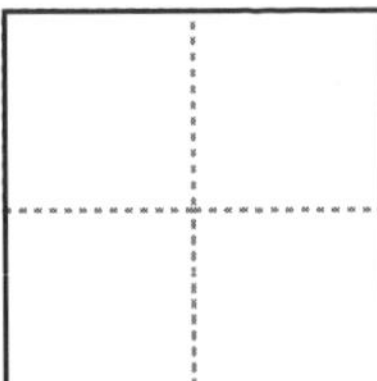

ライバル

***ra*ibaru**

rival

The expression "fight like cats and dogs" has a Japanese equivalent, but instead of a cat, the dog's rival is a monkey. The full expression is けんえんのなか (kenennonaka), which literally means "the relationship between a dog and monkey."

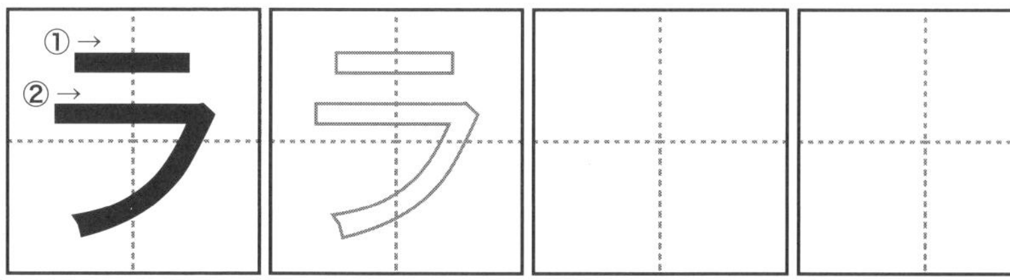

りゅう

***r*yu**

dragon

The dragons of Japanese legend closely resemble their Chinese counterparts, and are very fierce and powerful. Boys who are born during the たつどし (tatsudoshi; year of the dragon) are said to possess the characteristics that will make them leaders among men.

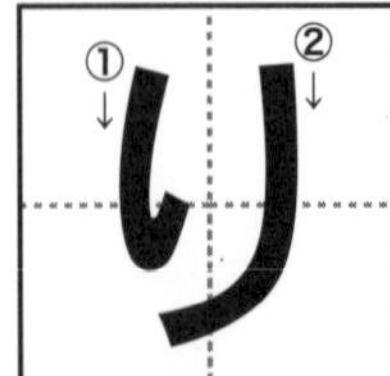

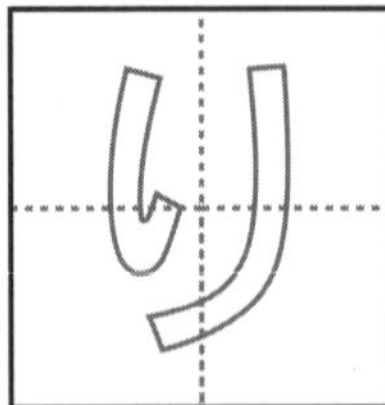

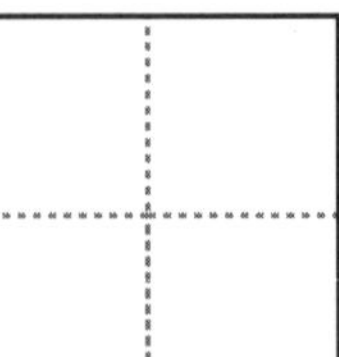

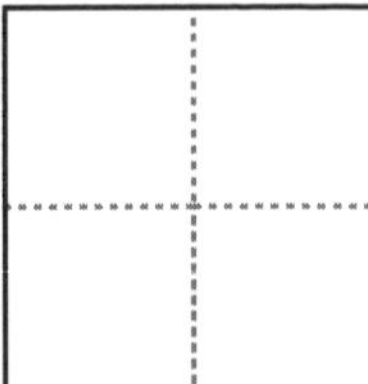

リサイクル

***ri*saikuru**

recycle

Tokyo's 28 million residents make it the most populous metropolitan area in the world. Remarkably, it is also one of the cleanest of all major cities, thanks in part to a comprehensive recycling program. In this picture, a young lady sorts garbage into three bins labeled プラスチック (purasuchikku; plastic), カン (kan; cans) and ビン (bin; bottles).

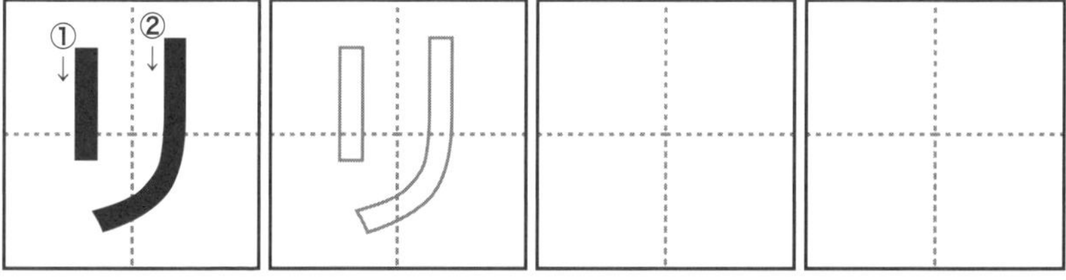

るいじ

***ru*iji**

similar

When you first started studying this book, you probably thought all hiragana and katakana looked the same. How about now? If you can tell the difference between characters such as る and ろ, and ク and ケ, you've just about mastered kana!

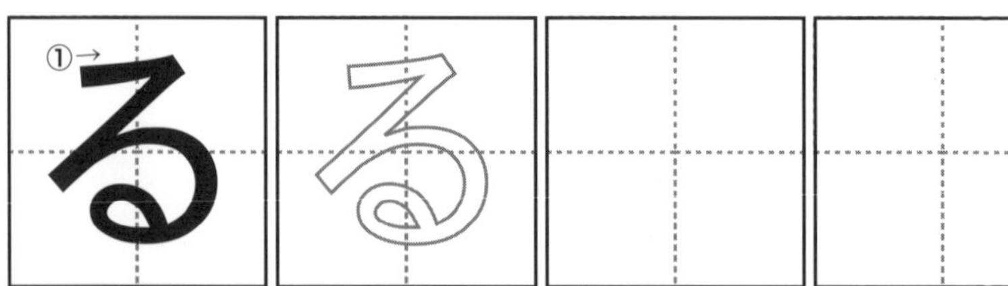

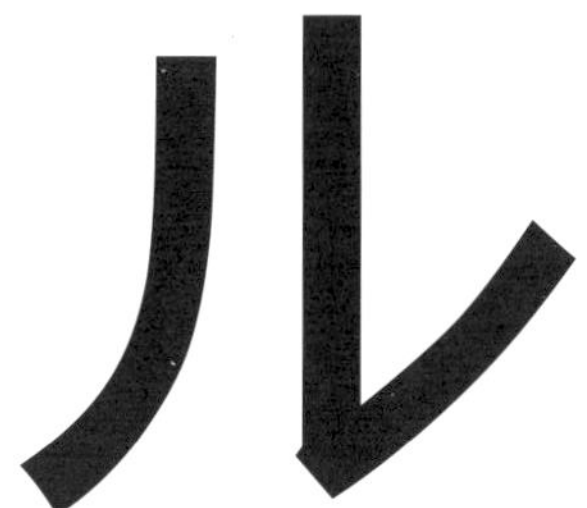

ルーペ

***ru*upe**

magnifying glass

There are several ways to say "magnifying glass" in Japanese, including むしめがね (mushimegane), which combines the words むし (mushi; insect) and めがね (megane; eyeglasses). The generic ルーペ derives from the German word "lupe."

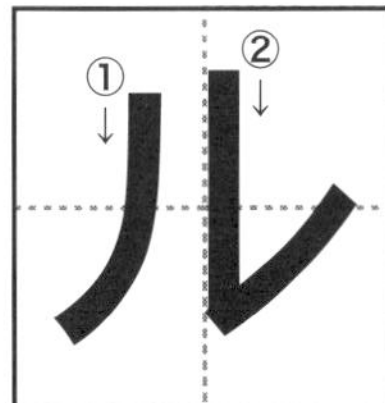

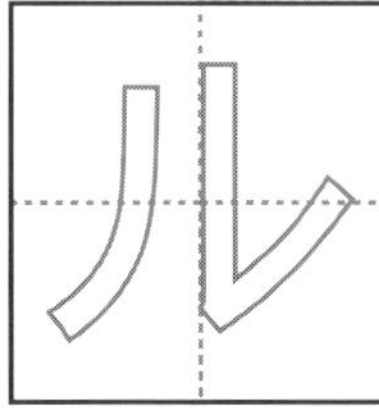

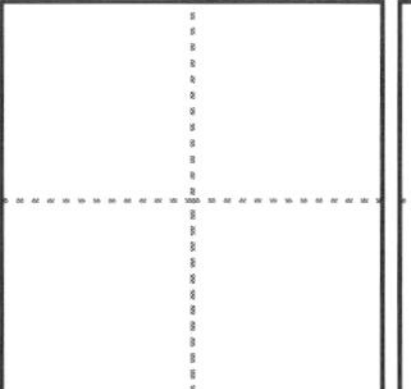

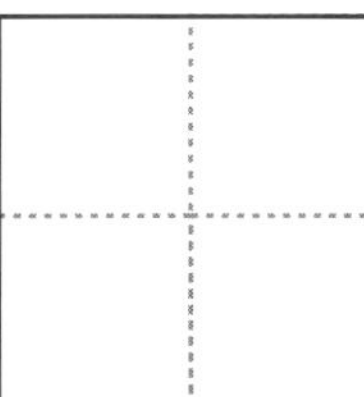

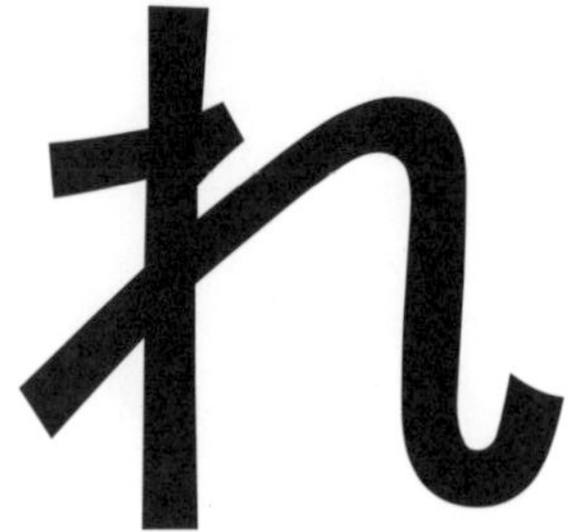

れいぞうこ

reizoko

refrigerator

Hungry for a late-night Japanese snack? Then climb out of bed and head to the refrigerator for some leftover なっとう (natto; sticky fermented soybeans), a few chunks of ばさし (basashi; raw horse meat), or maybe even a handful of deep-fried crickets. Oh, and don't forget the ぎゅうにゅう (gyunyu; milk).

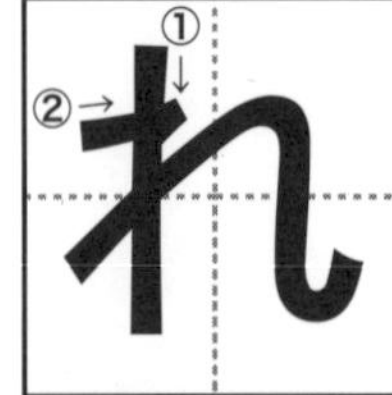

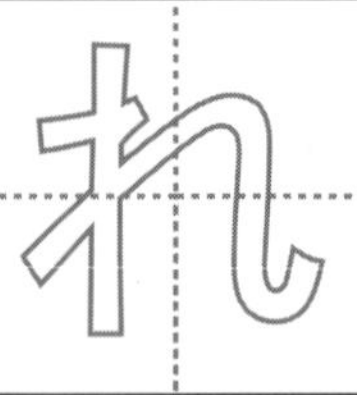

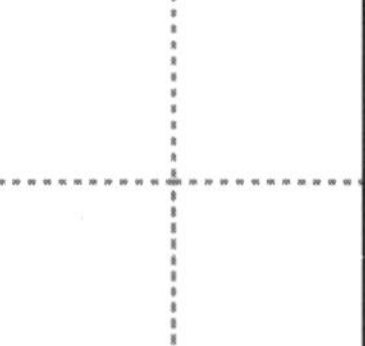

レインコート

reinkouto

raincoat

Planning to travel to Japan? Don't forget to pack a raincoat and かさ (kasa; umbrella). Tokyo alone gets an average of 60 inches of rain annually; other parts of the country are even wetter. Most of the downpours begin in early summer and culminate with the たいふう (taifu; typhoon) season in September.

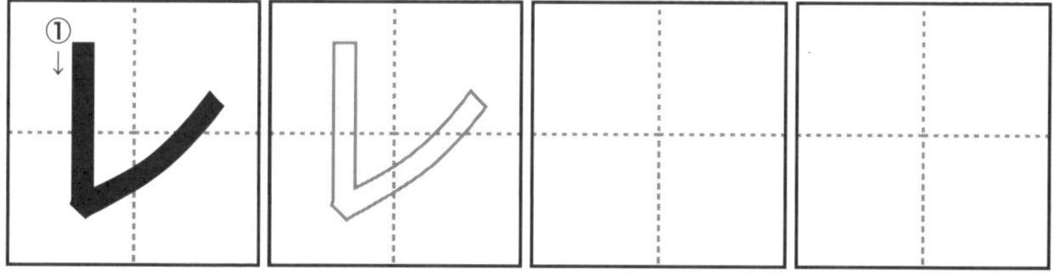

ろうそく

rosoku

candle

Nothing is more ロマンティック (romanchikku; romantic) than dining by candlelight with the one you love. The finest Japanese candles are made not from beeswax but rather wax from the はぜ (haze; Japanese wax tree).

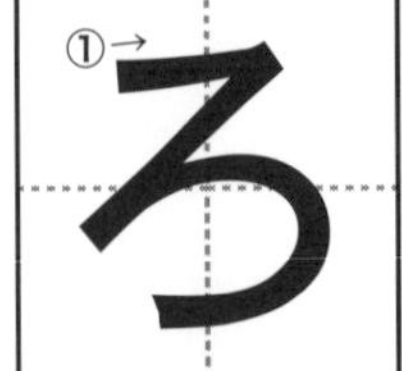

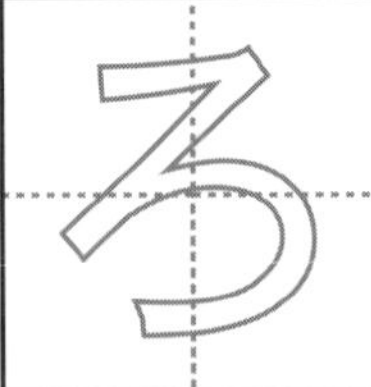

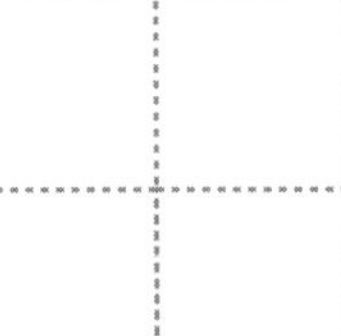

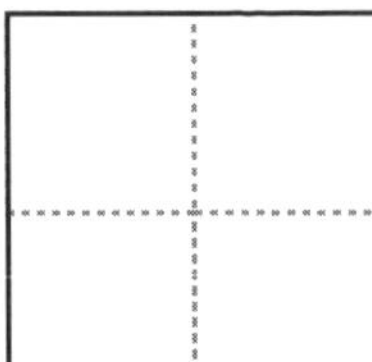

ロボット

***ro**botto*

robot

Japanese manufacturers have been making robot-type おもちゃ (omocha; toys) since the 1950s, when the first Robby the Robot windups were released. These sci-fi playthings have evolved over the years, and today Sony makes the highly sophisticated AIBO robotic dog. A brand-new AIBO costs about $2,000. An original Robby the Robot is now worth several times that amount.

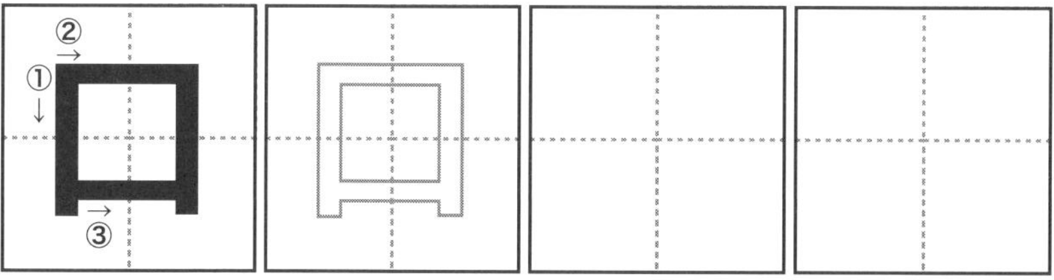

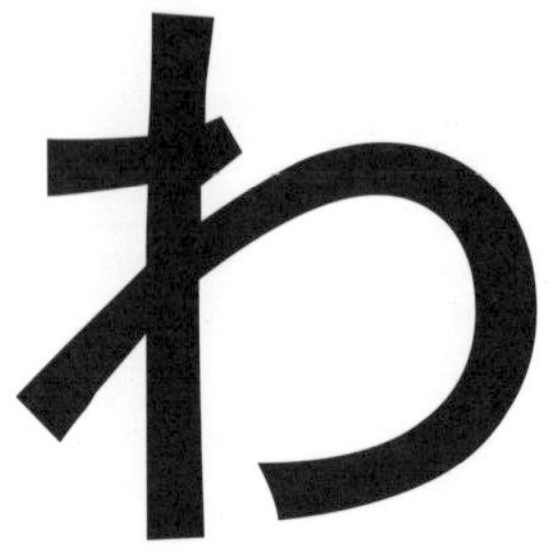

わらいごえ

***wa*raigoe**

laughter

Hey? What's so funny? Maybe someone just told him a わらいばなし (waraibanashi; humorous story). We hope he shares the じょうだん (jodan; joke) with us. The word for laughter combines わらい (warai; smile) with ごえ (goe; voice), and therefore can be interpreted as "smile with a voice."

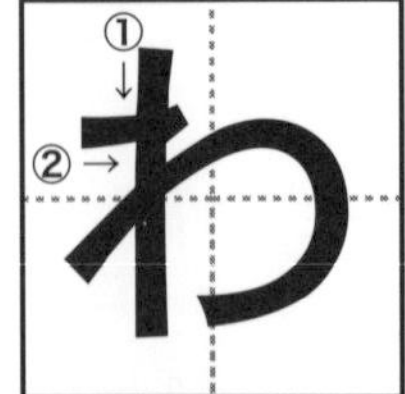

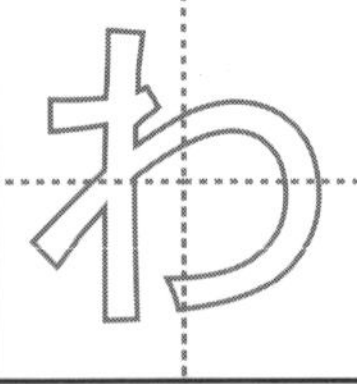

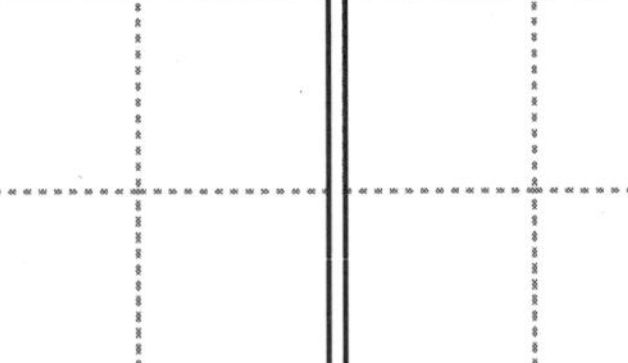

ワンピース

***wa*npiisu**

one-piece dress

The English word "one" is used often in Japanese. Some examples: ワンサイド (wansaido; one-sided), ワンマンショー (wanmansho; one-man show) and ワンステップずつ (wansuteppuzutsu; one step at a time).

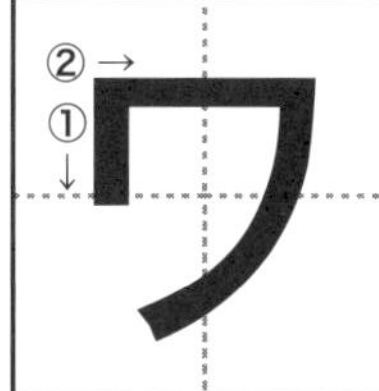

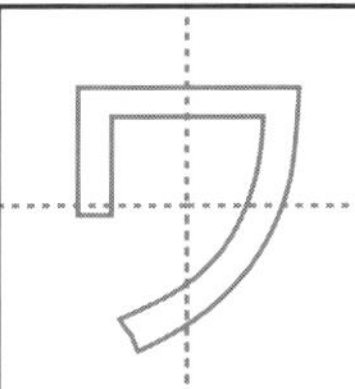

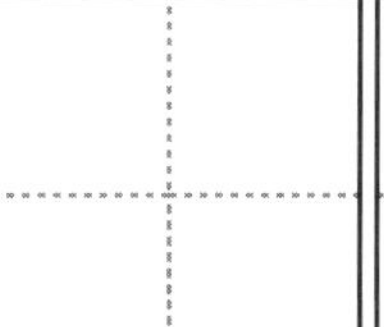

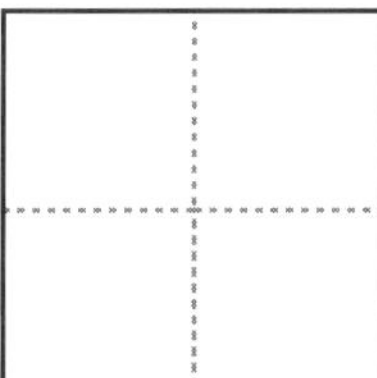

This character, romanized as "o" but pronounced either "o" or "wo," is used strictly as a particle, as in the phrase ほんをよむ (hon o yomu; read a book), where ほん (hon) means book, よむ (yomu) is the verb "to read" and を is the particle.

The ん character is pronounced as "n" or "m" and is the only consonant sound in which a Japanese word can end (for example, ほん, hon; book). This kana also can be used in the middle of a word, though never at the beginning.

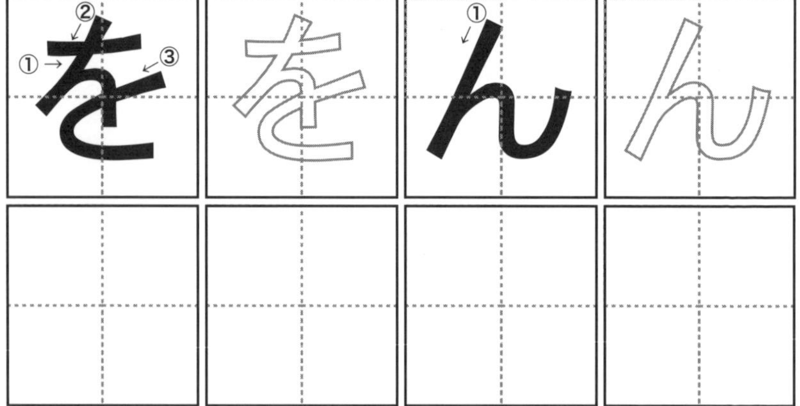

The katakana equivalent of the hiragana particle を is almost never used in formal Japanese writing. We present the kana here for reference only.

The same rules that govern the use of the hiragana ん also apply to ン in katakana. It is the only consonant sound to appear at the end of a word, and is never used at the beginning of one.

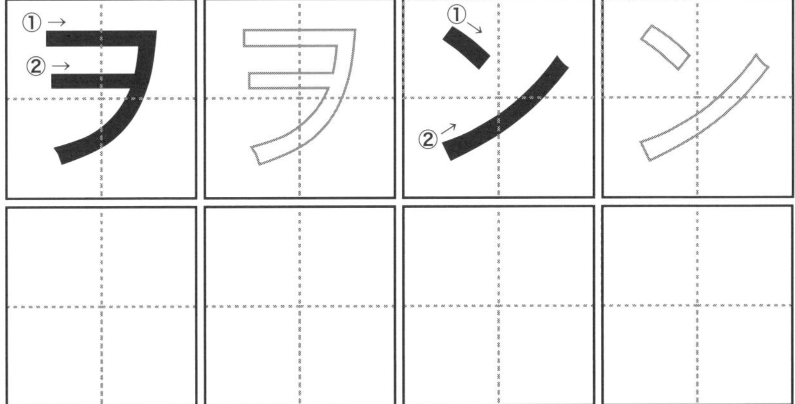

PRACTICE SECTION

GLENN KARDY is the editor of several volumes in the renowned *How to Draw Manga* series of art-instruction guides, including *Getting Started*, the first book of its kind to be used at major universities in both the United States (UCLA) and Japan (Waseda). Glenn lives in the Tokyo suburb of Kawaguchi City with his wife, their daughter and a collection of Oakland A's bobblehead dolls.

CHIHIRO HATTORI, niece of legendary manga artist Eiichi Fukui, was a graphics designer at Tokyo-based TechnoArt before turning her attention full-time to her manga career. Chihiro and her husband live in Yokohama, where they enjoy fine food, fast cars and high fashion.

Cover illustrations by Chihiro Hattori
Front cover CG color by You Garmendia Ayala
Back cover CG color by Honepanda
Project coordinator: Kanako Umehara